BOOKS BY JOHN LANGONE:

Vital Signs: *The Way We Die in America*
Life at the Bottom: *The People of Antarctica*
Long Life: *What We Know and Are Learning About the Aging Process*

FOR CHILDREN:

Death is a Noun: *A View of the End of Life*
Goodbye to Bedlam: *Understanding Mental Illness and Retardation*
Bombed, Buzzed, Smashed, or . . . Sober? *A Book about Alcohol*
Human Engineering: *Marvel or Menace?*

Long Life

Long Life

*What We Know and Are Learning
About the Aging Process*

by John Langone

Little, Brown and Company   Boston   Toronto

FIRST EDITION

T 11/78

Library of Congress Cataloging in Publication Data

Langone, John, 1929–
  Long life.

  Includes index.
  1. Aging. 2. Rejuvenation. 3. Longevity
I. Title.
QP86.L36   612.6'7   78-17349
ISBN 0-316-51428-4

Lines on page 234 from "The Road Not Taken" from THE POETRY
OF ROBERT FROST edited by Edward Connery Lathem. Copyright
1916, © 1969 by Holt, Rinehart and Winston. Copyright 1944 by Robert
Frost. Reprinted by permission of Holt, Rinehart and Winston, Pub-
lishers, and the Estate of Robert Frost.

Designed by D. Christine Benders

*Published simultaneously in Canada
by Little, Brown & Company (Canada) Limited*

PRINTED IN THE UNITED STATES OF AMERICA

For Josephine, my mother

Acknowledgments

IN A BOOK of this sort, a synthesis if you will, it is customary to cite the author's source materials by chapter and verse. But because I view that approach as somewhat forbidding — and best left, for better or worse, to more definitive and scholarly works — no footnotes or backnotes have been included. Instead, I have chosen to use oblique references throughout the text so as not to interrupt a narrative aimed at the general reader.

While my sources are too numerous to be fully cited, several should be mentioned here. Apart from material culled from scores of medical and scientific journals, from papers presented at research symposia, from background supplied me by information officers at universities, medical centers and research facilities, and from data gathered in personal interviews with numerous scientists, a good deal of the substance of this book came to me via two outstanding government agencies, The National Institute on Aging, and the Gerontology Research Center in Baltimore. Without their help, I could not have been apprised easily of current attitudes toward aging and of the status of the many research projects under way in gerontology.

Among the many books and publications consulted are these: *The Hermetic and Alchemical Writings of Paracelsus,* translated by Arthur Edward Waite (James Elliott and Co., London, 1894); *Astrology and Alchemy* by Mark Graubard (Philos Library, 1953); *The Youth Doctors* by Patrick M. McGrady, Jr. (Coward-McCann, 1968); *The Sources of Life* by Serge Voronoff (Bruce Humphries, Inc., Boston, The Ryerson Press, Toronto, 1943); *The Hormone Quest* by Albert Q. Maisel (Random House, 1965); *Sex and Life: Forty Years of Biological and Medical Experiments* by Eugen Steinach (Viking, 1940); *Treatise on Health and Long Life* by Luigi Cornaro (translated from the Italian, edition of 1612); *The Prolongation of Life* by Elie Metchnikoff, English translation by P. Chalmers Mitchell (G. P. Putnam's Sons, 1908); *The Life of Elie Metchnikoff* by Olga Metchnikoff (Houghton Mifflin, 1921); *Biological Time* by P. Lecomte du Noüy (Macmillan, 1933); *Human Destiny* by P. Lecomte du Noüy (Longman's, Green & Co., 1937); Ana Aslan, in *Die Therapiewoche* (Vol. 7, No. 13, Oct. 1956); "The Effects Produced by Man on Subcutaneous Injections of a Liquid Obtained from the Testicles of Animals" by Charles-Édouard Brown-Séquard (presented June 1, 1889, before the Société de Biologie de Paris); *Brown-Séquard's Own Account of His Famous Alleged Remedy for Debility and Old Age,* edited by Newell Dunbar (J. B. Cupples Co., Boston, 1889); *History of Medicine* by Fielding H. Garrison (W. B. Saunders Co.).

Dr. Alexander Leaf's reports on long-lived population groups, which appeared in the journals *Hospital Practice* and *Scientific American* (1973), were invaluable. So, too, were those by Vladimir Kyucharyants of the Novosti Press Agency and Zhores A. Medvedev in *The Gerontologist* (Oct. 1974). For background on Paul Niehans's cellular therapy, I consulted, among other publications, the *Journal of the American Medical Association* (Feb. 13, 1960) and articles in *Today's Health* (Walter S. Ross, Oct. 1970, and Bard Lindeman, June 1975). The Boston University publication *Boston Medical Quarterly* (June 1964) was the source for the study of Boston's Chinese community by Drs. S. C. Chen and Joyce Liu Chen.

I am deeply indebted to Drs. Denham Harman and Johan Bjorksten for the many reprints they sent me to explain their respective theories of free radicals and cross-linkage, to the Salk Institute for Biological Studies in San Diego for material relative to the work of Dr. Leslie E. Orgel on the error theory of aging, and to the Gerontological Society for furnishing me with copies of Leonard Hayflick's Kleemeier Lecture (1973) on cell doubling and other publications on this most fascinating concept. *Medical World News*'s reports on "Hayflick's Limit" and Hayflick's own report in the *New England Journal of Medicine* (Dec. 2, 1976) were also most helpful.

My thanks also to Duke University's Center for the Study of Aging and Development, to Sandoz Pharmaceuticals for a transcription of its panel discussion on "Where Does Aging Begin?" and to the American Medical Association for the proceedings of its 1974 Congress on Improving the Quality of Life in Later Years.

Lastly, I am indebted to my science-writing colleagues, who by their articles and books, alerted me to many things I might have overlooked, to the Harvard Medical School's Francis A. Countway Library of Medicine and the Widener Library, and to my most capable editor, William D. Phillips, without whose patience and guidance this book could not have taken shape.

John Langone

Hingham, Massachusetts
March, 1978

Contents

Part I

Time's Winged Chariot

Chapter One

I CAN RECALL VIVIDLY my thirtieth birthday. We threw a big house party and invited all my friends, each of whom was slightly younger than I. It was long before Gail Sheehey outlined her passages through midlife crises, to depress as well as uplift us all. But I knew the feeling of being pigeonholed, even then, and I spent that evening getting more depressed with each drink, bemoaning this pass to which I had come, wailing for anyone who would take me seriously (none did) that thirty was what all of us reporters put at the end of our copy, it really did mean The End.

Damp eyed, I quoted Shakespeare and those gloomy lines about sans teeth, sans eyes, sans everything, throwing in a bit from the Koran that I had learned as a youth, something to the effect of wishing that I could bolt the door against age, tell him I wasn't home and to come back another time. I recall remarking that all the airline stewardesses were starting to look like high school cheerleaders, and that I couldn't idolize the big league pitchers anymore because they were all such tender kids, not the way they used to be, all paunchy and bullnecked and older than I. I sang "Backward turn backward, O Time in thy flight," and "I'd give all my tomorrows for one yesterday."

Today, in my late forties, though I still worry about my mortality, thankfully I have not yet run down. But I am changing, despite all of that, as we all change as we age, and I am aware that something within me is steadily ticking away my hours, aging my cells and organs at different rates, forcing me to become less efficient in mind and body. I was correct in being aware of my aging at thirty, although I confused it then, as we all do at thirty, with being aged. Aging is not simply a condition that belabors the elderly. It is a process that begins, biologically speaking, at the moment of conception and gains momentum when we reach the peak of our growth period, moving us relentlessly toward our allotted Biblical threescore and ten, with perhaps a bit more thrown in as a bonus for having the right genetic programming in our cells, or the right dietary habits, environment, job, and mental attitude. While we are not born old, we are aging from birth, and the youth who insists that he or she is not old should be asked the question, Compared to whom?

Some of the changes that occur in me now are noticeable; others, too subtle to be felt or seen at the moment, will become evident during the sixth decade. Within me already, since I entered my twenties, in fact, there is a slowup in the production of hormones, those gland-spawned chemical secretions that determine just about everything from personality to sexual behavior to how fast the heart beats. In my thirties, that heart was not pumping blood as easily, and my lungs, with arterial links to the heart, are not taking in as much oxygen as they once did. By the time I am eighty, the amount of blood pumped by my heart each minute will have fallen by about forty percent. While I was an infant in my mother's arms, my average pulse beat per minute was around 130. But when I reach sixty it will be somewhere around 67 to 80. With advancing age, kidney and bladder function diminishes by fifty percent, arteries become less resilient, fat deposits increase around the heart, and body temperature drops. The basal metabolic rate — the pace at which we expend energy while at rest — decreases.

There are other symptoms of this gradual wasting process as the clock ticks inexorably on, moving us all toward a time of youth truly passed, the play's last act. My skin, for example, is not as tight as it was before, especially under the eyes and the chin and in the jowls. I wonder, as I look into my mirror early in the morning, when I have gotten wearily out of bed and gone slowly into the harsh, telling light of the bathroom, whether I will have to wear glasses to cover up the bags, and turtlenecks and a beard to hide the sag of flesh that will come. We are growing old together, I say to my mirror image, you and I. It was good in one way, I think, that John Kennedy went out at such an age, even in such a sudden way. Standing in front of this polished glass that is beginning to distort my long-held and comfortable impression of myself, I think that if I live to be eighty I will still remember JFK, handsome and forty-five, vibrant, alive, died a youth not an old man, never eighty. It's a nice way to be remembered by one's friends, especially if you're proud.

The clock ticks on, and we find we cannot read small type or hear whispered words as easily. The hair turns gray as follicles atrophy, and more clumps of it now wind up tight against the bathtub drain after a shower and shampoo. We steadfastly refuse to go into a larger waist size, preferring to suck in our stomachs painfully, particularly when teenagers enter the room. With increasing age, we grow shorter and, quite probably, stooped. Bones become brittle and lighter with osteoporosis, and we know we're getting there when the creaking noise we hear as we climb the stairs isn't coming from the stairs. We see our cheeks hanging from each side of the nose as we puff through pushups. Muscles shrink and lose their power, affecting not only work and play activities but the respiratory system and excretory functions as well. The brain, that organic computer infinitely more complex than the electronic brains it has devised and built, decreases in size and weight as thousands of its cells die and are not replaced, each and every day. By the time we reach seventy, it will be about half what it was. Eventually, that brain will become clogged with cellular debris that will cause cerebral arteriosclerosis with its intellectual deficits and disordered behavior and many other distressing changes, things like not remembering that you've told that story before to people who do.

Some people, and they are the fortunate ones, can see some humor in all of this, and they are the ones who never use words like inexorable when describing the aging process. Once, a friend of mine, a newspaper columnist, polled the office one day to get our opinions about when age starts creeping up. His list was both facetious and on the mark. When you notice that life insurance salesmen don't call as often. When you think it might be comfortable to decorate with reclining furniture. When it makes you feel goofy to chew bubble gum. If you sometimes get cravings for extinct foods, like Kellogg's Pep. If it's been a long time since anyone asked if you were a natural blond. When you would rather dress warmly than fashionably. When Groucho doesn't seem so old on the reruns. When salesladies stop calling you dear. When chocolate doughnuts become repulsive.

Frivolous yes, but also true. The fact is that aging is not something that happens to us in the distant future like the death which surrounds its outermost edges, something final that will happen in its own due time. We can and do feel age's encroachment fairly early, as I have said, and in fact we are experiencing it for more of our lives than not. Everything that lives seems to have its own built-in timer, with the clock set for different life spans. The bristlecone pine, the oldest living thing on earth, has managed to pass the 4,000-year mark, thriving in forest preserves in eastern California and on windswept ridges in Arizona, Utah, Nevada and Colorado. One California Bristlecone, appropriately named Methuselah, is 4,600 years old; another died at age 4,900 near Wheeler Peak in Nevada. The animal kingdom, however, is not so blessed. We are not bristlecone pines. Forced to be mobile to survive, we do not possess the ability to grow as slowly and almost indefinitely as do the long-lived pines that appear to live in a state of hibernation, their time clocks moving sluggishly. In general, the life span of a quick-maturing and active animal is shorter than that of a relatively passive animal having a longer maturation period. A fly might live for a day, a flea thirty days, a white rat four years, dogs and cats about twenty years, chimpanzees and horses about forty, a hippopotamus fifty, an Indian elephant eighty, freshwater mussels and some fish about one hundred, and large tortoises to better than one hundred and fifty years. Human beings, the longest-living mammals, mature physically in about twenty-five years to maximum body size and strength — with a limit somewhere around one hundred and fifteen years. One advantage we do have over the shorter-lived mammals, and the one that gives us a longer life span, is our slower maturation rate. Granted, it is not as slow as the aforementioned trees, but it is a factor. A monkey's brain, for example, reaches maximum development in six to twelve months from birth, while the human brain requires a quarter of a century. Human beings, because of this delay maturity, are unable to give up their dependence on mothers and family until long after, say, monkeys do. As a result, we are better able to adapt to our environment, moving slowly and surely toward a longer life than the other mammals who are forced from birth to fend almost immediately for themselves.

There are very marked differences in the way people

age. While some individuals are total wrecks at fifty, emotionally and physically, nearly all of us can point to a Picasso or some relative or friend who appears to have aged "successfully," who has led a healthy, happy, vigorous and contributory life. Studies have shown that many physiological characteristics are well maintained even in advanced age in some individuals; some eighty-year-olds' kidney function, for instance, may be as good as that of the average fifty-year-old.

All of which means that the effects of age are highly individual, that chronological age by itself is not a very good indicator of how well our bodies will work. Biological age — defined as the state reached by an organism at a definite period of life — is. But determining it is one of gerontology's nettling problems. If we could get an accurate determination of biological age — which, again, need not be the same as chronological age — this would be of obvious value for elderly persons seeking accurate information about the condition of their health and their functional capacity. If there were such a guide, physicians would be able to detect deviations from a range of normal function at certain ages, and possibly take appropriate remedial action. While the clock of aging itself would not be slowed with such an approach, the quality of life would surely brighten. But unfortunately, as one scientist remarked recently, "The method of determining the age of dogs, cattle and horses from the condition of the teeth cannot be applied to man."

It should be evident in this age of scientific sophistication that the standard dictionary definition of aging as being simply the present participle of age, and Shake-speare's description of the Seventh Age as "second childishness and mere oblivion," leaves much to be de-sired. So, too, does the jargon of the gerontologist — "A progressive unfavorable loss of adaptation and a decreas-ing expectation of life with the passage of time that is expressed in measurement as decreased viability and increased vulnerability to the normal forces of mortal-ity."

Indeed, it may not be possible to define aging in gen-eral terms beyond characterizing it as a slow and steady bodily decline that ends possibly in senility, and in death. But while it may defy definition, I am keenly aware as a science journalist who has covered a broad range of medical topics over a good many years that this thing we call aging, this ripening, this harbor of all ills, this caricature of what we were, is a legitimate topic for careful scientific scrutiny. Today, in laboratories and universities throughout the world, teams of researchers have immersed themselves in the challenging field of gerontology, turning their attention, in ways that were not possible in the days when science was more naïve to the causes and effects of aging, to the progressive changes that occur in cell, tissue, organ and organism. The work is elegant, sophisticated, particularly that of the biochemists who labor for a fuller understanding of the mechanisms of cellular function and breakdown. For it is these mechanisms that are behind the changes our mirrors and our cameras reflect so bluntly, that are at the heart of that ever so subtle, gradual awareness that we are not as young as we were yesterday, that time always moves and changes in one direction, forward. There is an air of optimism about gerontological research that tends to dispel, at least from time to time, the belief of humankind in general that there is little if anything we can do to halt the march of years.

While death itself will undoubtedly always be with us, no matter how strongly we rage against it, there is good reason to believe that our susceptibility to certain diseases of aging will not, that one day all of the ailments that are related to aging will be wiped out, giving us a healthier old age, at least, if not some extra years. That is the focus of geriatrics, the branch of gerontology that is concerned with the prevention and treatment of the diseases that beset the elderly. Apart from this disease-oriented approach to solving the problems of aging, there are the other, more difficult, attempts to actually arrest the aging process itself, to slow down the clock, giving us more of the time we all wish we had. Such research treats aging as a purely biological phenomenon that affects all animal species. This is intrinsic, "pure," aging that I am now talking about, that built-in obsolescence in our body's cells that kills us a little more each day. But locating the clock within us that ticks off our personal hours and years, measuring them out to us the way an hourglass gives up its grains of sand, is not a simple task. Some gerontologists are convinced there is one central clock of aging in the brain; others are certain there are clocks in each cell. Still others throw the whole notion of a biological clock out the window, arguing that there may not be any such thing as an aging process tied to a key cellular phenomenon and applicable to all species. Rather, they feel that what we regard as aging is simply a composite of many different mechanisms, biological, sociological and psychological. One may grow "old" faster after a falling out with relatives and friends, for example, or after suddenly adopting a sedentary life after years of activity. Moving to a strange, new environment may do it, and so, too, may poor psychological adjustment to events such as the onset of baldness and sexual decline.

There are, doubtless, areas of overlap, and no responsible scientists can deny that we are the product of both our heredity and environment. Yet, when one talks of laboratory efforts to slow the rate at which we age, biochemistry is what is meant. And there is no ignoring that it may hold the secret to longevity. That branch of science can be regarded as the latest manifestation of an ancient human preoccupation, and its practitioners are the descendants of the wizards and alchemists who quested unceasingly for immortality and rejuvenation, both to be found, they thought, in some mysterious *elixir vitae*.

This book is not a do-it-yourself handbook on how to attain youth and long life in five easy steps, though the reader will be able to draw some conclusions about the benefits of proper diet, exercise, frame of mind and lifestyle. It is also not a definitive work on gerontological research. For one thing, there are nearly as many theories about aging as there are researchers, and for another I do not purport to be more than a science journalist skimming the cream, as it were, from a huge trough of hypotheses, experimental data and conclusions. Rather, this book is about the modern-day quest after an age-old dream, a science story to be sure, but one told with as few of the murky scientific details as possible. It is not written for the scientist, but it is about them and the more interesting things they do and suggest as they attempt to forestall the inevitable. It is also about the very real possibility that science may never ever do much about halting the process which, like death, is always with us. But whether or not science does succeed in markedly extending our life spans — and though a thousand-year-old human sounds somewhat improbable at this stage, one has to admit that science has given us many surprises over the years — one fact is quite clear. Whether the elderly are with us longer because we have wiped away their diseases or slowed their biological clocks, they deserve all the attention we, laypersons and scientists, can devote to improving their lot.

Chapter Two

It must be so — Plato, thou reason'st well! —
Else whence this pleasing hope, this fond desire,
This longing after immortality?
Or whence this secret dread, and inward horror,
Of falling into naught?
Why shrinks the soul
Back on herself, and startles at destruction?
                    — Joseph Addison (1672–1719)

THROUGHOUT THE HISTORY of civilization, human beings have longed for a never-fading world, for an imperishable home, an eternity of pleasure where there is no room for death. Immortality. Most of us have wished that it could be so, for the longest life, in truth, is short. This immortal longing is universal, and it is an important element in nearly all early cults and in all of the higher religions. References to it abound, and the very foundation of Christianity is faith in the resurrection of man on the last day, body and soul. Cave paintings and sculptured figurines of the Stone Age many thousands of years before Christ attest to a simple concept of life after death. There is archaeological evidence that Cro-Magnon man, the prototype of modern European man, who roamed the earth between 60,000 and 10,000 B.C., believed that the cave paintings of animals he had killed in the hunt held their souls. For the Aztecs, the souls of warriors slain in battle as well as those of women who died in childbirth went to the sun, and savages of Borneo thought there were seven souls in every man, that they flew from the body at death through the big toe, in the shape of a butterfly. Other peoples believed the souls of friends and relatives lingered near the scene of their former lives, depending on the living for food and remembrance. In Greek burial custom, wine was poured on the grave to quench the thirst of the dead, and animals were sacrificed for the soul's food. Only the kindest terms were used to describe the deceased during the banquet in his honor, because it was believed that the soul was present at the feast. The Buddhist's Eightfold Path of Righteous Living takes the believer through a long chain of rebirths, both plant and animal, to Nirvana, variously regarded as the extinction of individual passion and hatred, and as a state of holiness, perfect peace and wisdom. There is the Muslim's Heaven of Sensual Delight, and the Greeks' place of bliss, the Elysian Fields, located by Homer on the western border of the earth. We have the Icelandic saga of the man who shed his skin every score of years and ended up thirty years old each time, and the myth of Phoenix flapping renewed from the fiery ashes of its nest of spices. In a famous dialogue, *Phaedo,* written about the fourth century B.C.,

Plato discussed the immortality of the soul and its ability to be reborn again and again. He argued that everything in nature followed cycles and patterns: heat became cold, cold became heat, people went to sleep, they woke up. It was right to assume that this same kind of cycling applied to dying and returning to life, Plato argued. Just as the living died, so, too, did the dead come back to life. If this were not the case, said the philosopher, life would soon disappear from the universe.

Guarantees of the soul's immortality, however, were not enough for all of the ancients. Like most of us they had moments when they tired of putting their trust in blind faith and bargaining with nebulous saints. Prayer's delivery system is often sluggish and it usually works, as football coach Frank Lahey used to say, when the players are big. Very early, there was a need for more direct access to youth and long life, possibly even immortality, and so the myths and legends of rejuvenation sprang up, some ludicrous, some pseudoscientific, but all brimming with hope and vitality. There was always something that one could swallow or sprinkle about or rub on or immerse one's self in that would smooth the body's wrinkles and confer longer or lasting life. And so, we have the Fountain of Youth on storied Bimini, the object of quest by Ponce de León, Narvaez and De Soto, reputedly found elsewhere by Sir John Mandeville, author of a famous fourteenth-century book of travels, who proclaimed grandly afterward: "And thei that duellen there and drynken often of that Welle, thei never had syknesse, and thei semen alle ways young. I have drinken thereof three or four sithes, and yit, methinkethe, I fare better."

Morgan Le Fay's Ring of Ogier that removed the infirmities of age, the Wood of the True Cross used by Constantine's mother to revive a dead man, the Holy Grail and its rewards for the absolutely pure, the Indian mrtasamjivani plant, the rare herb that obliterated old age and death. Some of the recipes for earthly renewal were more drastic than rubbing a ring, touching a chalice, or swallowing an herbal brew, and we read in Ovid's *Metamorphoses* of the sorceress Medea's remedy for the affliction that is age — a transfusion.

> Medea plunged the dagger in the old man's throat
> To drain his blood; then in his gaping veins
> Instilled her magic brew, which filled his feeble
>   age
> With strength he had not known for ninety years.

But whether conferred by talisman or immersion in a magical spring, youth was easy to come by, at least according to the legends, and when a seeker had no direct access to such potent rejuvenators, the simplest and most common way of getting restored was to find the right person and merely ask. Miracle-working relics brought fame and wealth to many monasteries and churches as hordes of crippled, sightless and otherwise maimed believers sought and bought the opportunity to touch corpse of saint or bit of his or her bone, and kneel before a vial of Christ's blood lighted by the very candle the angel of the Lord set in His tomb.

Where the monks and their holy relics failed to deliver, which was often, the alchemists stepped in to fill the gap, toiling in steaming, foul-smelling laboratories in search of that which would stay the arrival of the two universal enemies, old age and death. Amid a stinking clutter of queer decoctions, quintessences, infusions, pastes and potions, electuaries, tinctures, butters and metallic dusts, these medieval pseudoscientists pressed their hunt for the ultimate vivifying agent, the *lapis philosophorum*, the Philosophers' Stone, that ill-defined, soluble substance possessing power to change base metals into gold and silver, and bestow perpetual youth and good health. Its dual potential was based on the assumption that since the stone was capable of purging a metal's impurities so that it could be turned into a more precious substance, so could it cleanse a body of the impurities and defects that come with aging. The alchemists' belief that a common metal could be transformed at all stemmed from their discovery of some simple chemical reactions, such as the deposition of copper on iron when the latter is immersed in a solution of salts, a reaction they took to mean that iron had been changed into copper. They also noticed that after water was boiled for a long time, solids were deposited on the bottom of the vessel. This forced the alchemists to assume that if copper could be raised from iron, and water turned to earthy material, then gold, the highest and most potent of mineral entities, must also be within their reach.

Full of obfuscation and mystical humbuggery, the alchemists' formulas were more often than not a muddle of astrology, magic, superstition, and an involved view of the cosmos. Spirits dwelt in all things, and these could be extracted by fiery heat. Seven heavenly bodies — the sun, moon, Mars, Mercury, Jupiter, Saturn and Venus — corresponded to the seven known metals: gold, silver, iron, quicksilver, tin, lead and copper. Moreover, the alchemists believed, since the sun ruled the heart, the moon the brain, Jupiter the liver, Saturn the spleen, Mercury the lungs, Mars the bile, and Venus the kidneys, the seven planetary metals and their compounds were effective against diseases of those organs because of the influence of the stars. The Philosophers' Stone itself had a symbolic as well as a physical significance. It stood for the highest wisdom that humankind could attain; it was perfection, fulfillment, purification of the soul. The alchemists' laboratory labors were also a religious ceremony paying homage to their belief that the chemical composition of the human body was inextricably linked to the cosmos; transmuting lead to gold was more than chemistry, it was a ritualistic process by which the alchemist could demonstrate, with tangible results in a caldron or flask, the validity of his perception of the universe. As he sought the means of converting lesser metals to gold, so, too, was he seeking to transmute his own imperfect body and psyche. Thus, for the alchemists, gold-making was not, contrary to the generally held opinion, the chief end of the search for the stone. The precious yellow metal was both a potent curative for physical ailments — its power as an arcanum was believed to surpass that of all other substances — and a representation of humanity brought to the loftiest spiritual plane. "*Aurum nostrum non est aurum regi,*" intoned an alchemist's creed. "Our gold is not the gold of everyone." For those who took this borderline science seriously, who heard the ticking of the biological time clock and tried to do something about slowing its steady movement, alchemy was the celebration of a high and holy Mass, and the laboratory was its altar.

But, it had its share of quacks, and its snake-oil salesmen: Leonhard Thurnheysserzum Thurn, a Swiss goldsmith's apprentice who sold "gold bricks" made of gold-plated tin and horoscopes and secret potions that cured all manner of ailments; John of Gaddesden who prescribed ivory turnings for failed memories; John Bates and his "cardiac waters," and the "tablets of magnanimity" which reportedly restored the aged to sexual potency. And bizarre recipes compounded of such diverse ingredients as tigers' testicles, rooster genitals, senna and dill. "Pulverize and pass through a sieve," said one, "an ounce of soccotrine aloes, one drachm of zedoary, one drachm of gentian, one of the finest saffron, one of the finest rhubarb, one of white agaric, one of Venice treacle, one of kina, and place in a bottle, add a pint of good brandy, place whole in shade for nine days, shaking it in the morning and evening. Open on tenth day, add more brandy, filter." The concoction, promised the inventor, "transforms the body, removes its harmful parts, its incompleteness, and transforms its crudity into a pure, noble and indestructible being."

There were other variations, such as the *elixir proprietatis,* a mixture of aloes, saffron and myrrh in vinegar and stirred "according to the ancients' formulation into a vivifying and preserving balsam, able to continue health and long life to its utmost limits." Borrowing on occasion from earlier Chinese and Indian recipes for immortality, the alchemists pulverized pine nuts, resin, pearls, sapphires and cinnebar (mercury ore), extracted the juices of trees, flowers and vipers (the last based on an Indian legend that certain tribes lived to be four hundred years old by drinking an ounce of "viper waters" every morning on an empty stomach for fifteen days each year during the springtime), and compounded these ingredients into balms, charms, amulets, elixirs and inhalants, or poured them into mineral baths. So intent were they in their hot pursuit that it is doubtful they would have been deterred had they known that seven Chinese rulers who tried similar rejuvenators on themselves during the T'ang dynasty (A.D. 618–907) died from the effects.

Perhaps the greatest, certainly the most flamboyant, alchemist of the day was a Swiss whose real name was Theophrastus Bombastus von Hohenheim (1493–1541). He took the *nom de plume* Philippus Aureolus Paracelsus to imply he was greater than a renowned physician and writer named Celsus. Son of a physician, Paracelsus learned alchemy in the mines and smelters of the Tirol, astrology and folk medicine from gypsies, executioners, barbers and midwives, and medicine of a relatively high order from his father's library and at Ferrara under Leonicenus, a famed translator of Hippocrates. Bombast in more than name, Paracelsus was the self-styled *Philosopher of the Monarchia, Prince of Spagyrists, Chief Astronomer, Surpassing Physician and the Trismegistus of Mechanical Arcana.* In one of his frequent loud bursts of fustian, he roared on the pages of his *Hermetic and Alchemical Writings*: "I have been chosen by God to extinguish and blot out all the phantasies of elaborate and false works of delusive and presumptuous words, be they the words of Aristotle, Galen, Avicenna, Mesua or the dogmas of any among their followers. . . . After me, you Avicenna, Galen, Rhasis, Montagnana and the others. You after me, not I after you. Follow me. It is not for me to follow you, for mine is the monarchy."

His lack of humility and his attacks on Galen's four humors — blood, phlegm, black and yellow bile, which supposedly determined one's physical and mental health — brought him the scorn and ridicule of his peers. If one can believe his early biographers, he looked like a drover, lived like a pig, was often drunk in his opinions and otherwise, and spent most of his time in the company of roistering, dissolute rabble. His labors at the laboratory bench for youth and vitality, it was whispered, were nothing more than a futile search for the genitals he reportedly lost at the hands of a drunken band of soldiers; his laboratory assistant was reputed to be a demon who lived in the hilt of his sword. "The profession disowned him as a degreeless quack," goes one account, "a reckless empiric, incapable of dissection and ignorant of anatomy. He returned the scorn of the doctors in the liveliest billingsgate. He laughed at their barbarous prescriptions, their silk shirts, finger rings, sleek gloves and haughty gait; he challenged them to come out of the classrooms into the chemical laboratory, to put on their aprons, soil their hands with the elements and, bending over furnaces, learn the secrets of nature by experiment and the sweat of their brows." After one biting bit of criticism of his ways, he observed sneeringly, "All the universities and all the old writers put together are less talented than my ass."

Paracelsus, too, heard the ticking of the clock of aging, and he worked unceasingly to find a way to gum up its works. At one point he claimed to have discovered an elixir that would do just that: "Take of mineral gold, or of antimony, very minutely ground, one pound. Of circulated salt, four pounds. Mix them together and let them digest for four months in horse dung. Thence will be produced a water, whereof let the pure potion be separated from that which is impure. Coagulate this into a stone, which you will calcine with cenifated wine. Separate again and dissolve upon marble. Let this water putrefy for a month, and thence will be produced a liquid in which are all the signs as in the first entity of gold or of antimony. Whereof, with good reason, we call this the first entity of these things."

Paracelsus had further instructions on how this preparation was to be used, all of which did little to improve his image as a hard-drinking quacksalver: "Let either of those first entities be put into a good wine, in such quantity that it may be tinged therewith. Having done this, it is prepared for this regimen: Some of the wine must be drunk every day, about dawn, until first all of the nails fall off from the fingers, afterwards from the feet, then the hair and teeth, and lastly the skin be dried up and a new skin produced. When all of this is done, that medicament or potion must be discontinued. And again, new nails, hair and fresh teeth are produced, as well as the new skin and all diseases of the body and mind pass away."

Despite his elixirs, Paracelsus was unable to preserve his own life, and he died at the age of forty-eight, reportedly of injuries sustained in a tavern brawl in Salzburg. But he was probably the one person through whom alchemy proper reached its highest point; for after him, the practice sank briefly into a more bizarre form of necromancy and pseudoscience before it was recovered and moved on to what we know today as chemistry. His writings and his formulas must be read cautiously because, in a sense, Paracelsus was a lab technician turned loose, and it is often difficult to determine where his muddling ended and his calculation began. Still, the odd scientific beat to which he marched drove him on a correct course away from the humors theory of sickness and its treatment on to one linking the physical and the chemical processes in the organism. Insisting that medicine was a branch of chemistry and that to restore a person to health it was necessary to restore chemical equilibrium, he devoted himself to utilizing the great therapeutic potential in inorganic as well as organic substances. He introduced numerous medicines made from mercury, zinc, sulfur, lead, arsenic and iron, and he gave the world laudanum, opium. He prepared hydrogen by mixing iron filings with sulfuric acid, wrote the first treatise on miners' disease, first saw the association between severe thyroid deficiency and goiter, and was the first to notice geographical differences in disease.

Today, of course, science has proven that trace concentrations of several of the same elements that Paracelsus made a part of the standard books of drugs and drug formulas are vital as well as detrimental to human metabolism. Research has discovered, for example, that muscular weakness usually attributed to the aging process may be due to a dietary deficiency of potassium. Zinc, which Paracelsus described as "an elementary substance," is essential to growth and may also protect against high blood pressure; mercury, one of the alchemist's standbys, is both detrimental and beneficial, for not only is it toxic in excessive amounts when it turns up in our fish and other food supplies, but its salts are valuable as antiseptics, parasiticides, antisyphilitics and diuretics, and it may also, according to the most recent research, be essential to the human diet; sodium aurothiomolate, derived from gold, has been used to treat rheumatoid arthritis, auric bromide has been used to treat epilepsy, headache and as a sedative; manganese, chromium and vanadium are reputed to protect against atherosclerosis; antimony, a principal ingredient in Paracelsus's elixirs, is found in a wide variety of modern medicines that remove warts, act as emetics, and treat parasitic diseases; potassium sulfate (also called *specificum purgans Paracelsi*) is used as a laxative.

True, many of the impressive results achieved by Paracelsus and others of his trade came about serendipitously as they laboriously mixed, distilled, precipitated, calcified, sublimated, crystallized, cupelled and decocted their way toward the elusive Stone, groping blindly in their gloomy laboratories for the secret of longevity. Crossing and skirting the border separating responsible scientific experimentation from sorcery and fanciful dabbling, they managed to shake the foundations of fifteenth- and sixteenth-century establishment medicine to make the fledgling discipline they plied the precursor of modern pharmaceutical chemistry. Indeed, it has been said that alchemy was the sickly but imaginative infancy through which modern chemistry had to pass before it attained its majority and became a positive science. Unfathomable as some of their writings are, occasional gems of science do sparkle through all of the mystic principles, the arcana and archaei that made up their strange world. If anything, they drew together — and only too briefly — scientific, religious, and philosophical principles and applied this ideal blend in an attempt to solve humankind's most nettling problems. They were not successful in providing us with the secret of longevity, yet their approach, when stripped of its "spagyrism," certainly is no more preposterous, nor any less vigorous, than that employed by today's laboratory gerontologists. Quite possibly, Paracelsus even gave up the quest for the secret to long life, for he once observed: "This only is what we say: that for a long life the following is the best regimen: moderate diet. We do not give this in detail because it is known to every physician." I doubt that any clinician or researcher would fault that nor, I hope, one of his other pronouncements, "If I want to prove anything, I shall not do so by quoting authorities, but by experiment and by reasoning thereupon."

While the alchemists often made illogical inferences, they were not, like some of today's researchers, dull. Take, for example, some of the physicians who came along after Paracelsus, men such as Hermann Boerhaave

(1668–1738), "Professor of the Theory and Practice of Physic and Also of Botany and Chemistry in the University of Leyden," author of *Materia Medica, Or A Series of Prescriptions Adapted to the Sections of Practical Aphorisms Concerning the Knowledge and Cure of Diseases.* Long before our own acceptance of surrogate sex partners to treat sexual dysfunction, Boerhaave was suggesting to an old burgomeister of Amsterdam that he lie between two young girls, assuring him that he would recover his youth and his spirits afterward. The practice is called gerocomy, and it was around long before Boerhaave. The Bible's First Book of Kings mentions it: "Now King David was old, and advanced in years, and when he was covered with clothes he was not warm. His servants, therefore, said to him, Let us seek for our Lord, the king, a young virgin, and let her stand before the king, and cherish him, and sleep in his bosom, and warm our Lord the king. So they sought a beautiful young woman in all the coasts of Israel, and they found Abisag, a Sunamitess, and brought her to the king." But the king "did not know Abisag," although he slept with her, and his death occurs in the very next chapter of the book, gerocomy notwithstanding.

Gerocomy got its biggest boost many years after David with the discovery of an ancient Roman tomb bearing the following inscription:

AESCULAPIO ET SANITATI

L. CLODIUS HERMIPPUS

QUI VIVIT ANNOS CXV DIES V

PUELLARUM ANHELLITU

QUOD ETIAM POST MORTEM EJUS

NON PARUM MIRANTUR PHISICI

IAM POSTERI SIC VITAM DUCITE

Addressed to Aesculapius, god of medicine and healing, and to health, the epitaph pays homage to L.
Clodius Hermippus who lived to be 115 years and five
days, "with the aid of the breath of young women, much
to the amazement of his physicians." The inscription ad-
vises: "Lead your life accordingly."

The tomb became the subject of an eighteenth-
century treatise, *Hermippus Redivivus* (Hermippus
Renovated) by a physician named Cohausen who sub-
titled his work: *Or, The Sage's Triumph Over Old Age
and the Grave, Wherein, a Method is Laid Down for
Prolonging the Life and Vigour of Man, Including a
Commentary Upon An Ancient Inscription, In Which
This Great Secret is Revealed, Supported by Numerous
Authorities.* Although Cohausen treads often on some
precarious scientific ground, he is not about to dash the
conviction of every man over thirty-five — that the only
secret to attaining the harmony of mind and body so
essential to longevity is to be able to have any beautiful
woman eighteen and older that we desire. His observations have a place in every book on gerontology if only
as a mild diversion. Cohausen's "secret" is based on the
premise that exhaled air carries with it some essential
"particles" of the person who lets it out. If another person breathes in those particles, he or she will, according

to this line of reasoning, become charged with whatever it is that is exhaled, presumably some beneficial quality as well as disease. Carrying that further, Cohausen suggested that if an old man were to be surrounded for several hours with young people, he would have to take in their expelled air, air that was loaded with the very essence of youth. He calls attention to the case of Francis Secardi Hongo, Consul of Venice, who died at age 115 in 1702: "Being much addicted to the fair sex, he had in all five wives and 15 or 20 concubines, all of them young and beautiful women, by whom he had 49 sons and daughters, whom he educated with the utmost tenderness, and was constantly with them, as much as his business would permit. He was never sick; his sight, hearing, memory and activity were amazing. He walked every day about eight miles, his hair which was long and graceful became white by the time he was fourscore but turned black at a hundred, as did his eyebrows and beard at 112. At 110, he lost all of his teeth, but the year before he died he cut two large ones with great pain. The reader will easily discern that the point upon which I chiefly insist is his having continually young company about him, especially young women."

Our scribe also mentions an unnamed nobleman of France who made use of Hermippus's secret, keeping in his house, "under the pretense of a charitable care of their education, 10 or 12 young girls in whose company he was continually, and maintained himself thereby, in a full flow of health and spirits til he was upwards of 90." It is further reported that the unidentified nobleman might have survived some years longer "had not a scruple struck into his head that there was something of irreligion in this practice, upon which he dismissed his guardian angels, fell into a languishing state, and in a very few months died as much for the want of their breaths as his own."

Proceeding, at last, to Hermippus himself, Cohausen drives on with full literary license, speculating that he was the director of a college of virgins where the time was spent in hours of delightful indulgence, in cheerful conversation, games, good food, music and other diversions, all in a setting that might have given Hugh Hefner the idea for his celebrated mansion weekends. Each of the young women slept in rooms open at the top, as was Hermippus's, so that the vivifying maidens' breath would flow easily to the old man as he slept. The effect of such an environment, Cohausen speculates, could only be positive: "In a college like this, with such company, and under such regulations, where all the pupils are chaste as Diana's nymphs, fresh as spring, sweet as summer and harmless as winter, ever full of life and spirits, free from disease, cares or distractions of mind, easy in the tempers, affable in manners, fond of obliging, grateful when obliged, I can scarce imagine that any man could spend his time more agreeably than Hermippus, life freer from a sense of sorrow, or more remote from the shadow of death."

Cohausen concludes his narrative by revealing the method of an alchemist for distilling the "salubrious particles" of human breath: "In five beds in a small room let there lie five virgins under the age of 13, and of wholesome constitution; then in the spring of the year, about the beginning of the month of May, let there be a hole pierced through the wall of the chamber, through which let there be inserted the neck of a matrass [a long-necked vessel used for distilling], the body of the glass being exposed to the cold air without. It is easy to apprehend that, when the room is filled with the breath and matter perspired by these virgins, the vapours will continually pass through the neck of the matrass into the body of the vessel, when through the coldness of the circumambient air then will be condensed into a clear water, which is a tincture of admirable efficacy, and may be justly stiled an *elixir vitae*, since a few drops of it, given in the beginning of an acute distemper, resolves and disperses the morbidic matter."

Cohausen's account may well have been a put-on, or it may have been a genuine piece of quaint naïveté. But whatever it was, implicit in it are two notions, one of them held valid by today's gerontologists, the other not. The first of these is that an environment in which the elderly are not isolated from youth helps slow the psychological phase of aging, if not the biological, by making the person feel young by thinking with the young. The other is that through gerocomy, with all of the emotional and physical uplift that men and women may gain from an occasional evening of carnal knowledge with someone younger and more virile, youth can actually be restored through the organs of sex. The first premise is valid. The second is not. No one can deny that sex is a great restorer, and it may even add a few years to the life span when it lessens anxiety and tension and improves one's outlook on life. In the male, regular sexual intercourse may even hold down prostate congestion, a common misery over age fifty. But over the years, a number of male scientists owning both legitimate and dubious credentials became blindly preoccupied with the alleged vivifying powers leashed in the testes, and convinced themselves and those who bought their remedies that sexual potency was the key to youth and vim.

The experiments of another German, physiologist Arnold Adolphe Berthold of Göttingen, may well have touched off the subsequent wave of testicle transplants and injections of their contents, procedures that were the end result of all the fascination with sexual potency and were to become almost faddish. It was in 1848 that Berthold, who had made a reputation as a responsible scientist in such diverse pursuits as finding an antidote for arsenic poisoning and investigating male hermaphroditism and myopia, performed an experiment that escaped notice at the time. He successfully grafted the testicles of a cockerel into the abdominal cavity of a capon and watched in awe and delight as the formerly desexed rooster began chasing hens again. It all had something to do with an *innere Sekretion*, Berthold surmised. He was unaware that he was on the threshold of hormone therapy.

But it was the later work of a brilliant and nomadic French neurologist, Charles-Édouard Brown-Séquard (1817–1894), that gave greater impetus to the idea that rejuvenation and sexual vigor were closely linked, and stimulated (as well as hindered) subsequent research into the science of endocrinology. Brown-Séquard had earned a meager living in sundry ways: giving French lessons and practicing midwifery in New York at five dollars a case, fighting a cholera epidemic on his native Mauritius, and serving as a professor of physiology and pathology of the nervous system at Harvard. He was also professor of experimental medicine at the Collège de France, a post he held until his death. In one dramatic laboratory experiment that won him considerable notoriety, he successfully revived the decapitated head of a dog eight minutes after it had been severed from its body. He injected oxygenated blood into its arteries and called to it by name, whereupon, according to one report, it turned its eyes toward him as though recognizing the voice.

Another experiment, however, brought him most of the publicity that followed him through later life. Reporting before the Société de Biologie de Paris on June 1, 1889, Brown-Séquard, who was seventy-two at the time, began by suggesting that the seminal fluid contained substances which find their way into the bloodstream and bring strength to the nervous and other bodily systems. This was tied to an earlier theory that sexual excess wasted vital energy. *Coitus modicus excitat, coitus nimius debilitate,* was one way of putting it. (Moderate intercourse stimulates, very much weakens.) Eunuchs are generally debilitated, the scientist said, proof that the mind and body are adversely affected by absence of testes; the waste of semen through sexual abuse and masturbation, he added, also had ill effects. Given all that, Brown-Séquard concluded, an injection of semen into the blood of old men would give them back their lost physical and mental powers. He then went on to explain to the stunned audience of graybeards how he mixed the blood and semen from the testicles of dogs and guinea pigs with water, using as little water as possible to obtain maximum potency. Then, he reported, he gave himself ten subcutaneous injections of the stuff — two in his left arm, all the others in his lower limbs. The results of this self-experimentation were, if one believes Brown-Séquard, astounding. The very day after the first injection, he told the Société, several radical changes occurred. Foremost, he regained all of the strength he possessed years before and was impotent no longer. Moreover, considerable laboratory work hardly tired him, he said, and he was able to perform experiments for several hours — standing and feeling no need to sit down. He was also able to write on abstruse subjects after hours of hard lab work. "For more than 20 years, I have never been able to do as much," said Brown-Séquard. "My friends know that owing to certain circumstances and habits I have for 30 years, or 40 years, gone to bed very early and done my writing in the morning, beginning it generally between three and four o'clock. For a great many years, I had lost all power of doing any serious mental work after dinner. Since my first subcutaneous injections, I have very frequently been able to do such work, two, three, and one evening for nearly four, hours. For a natural impetuosity, and also to avoid losing time, I had until I was 60 years old, the habit of ascending and descending stairs so rapidly that my movements were rather those of running than walking. This had gradually changed, and I had come to move slowly up and down stairs, having to hold the banister in difficult staircases. After the second injection, I found that I had fully regained my old powers, and returned to my precious habits in that respect."

Brown-Séquard tested his limbs with a dynamometer to measure muscular power — a week before his experiment and again a month afterward. He found a decided gain in strength. He even measured, before and after the first injection, the jet of his urine, unabashedly reporting to the Société members: "The average length of the jet during the ten days that preceded the first injection was inferior by at least a quarter of what it came to be during the 20 following days. It is, therefore, quite evident that the power of the spinal cord over the bladder was considerably increased."

Later, when he ceased injecting himself, he noted a gradual, although rapid, return of the general state of weakness that had existed prior to the first inoculation. "This loss of strength," he said, "is an excellent counterproof as regards the demonstration of the influence exerted on me by the subcutaneous injection of a spermatic fluid."

Brown-Séquard's revelations were a sensation with the press, and he was soon besieged with requests for injections. The elderly men who petitioned him regarded him as the reincarnation of Ponce de León.

A few other experimenters claimed to have duplicated his results, using testicular extract from rabbits and pigs. Some time later, the Russian physiological chemist

Alexander von Poehl mass-produced what he called spermin, the supposed active ingredient in sperm, and had it marketed widely for treating males suffering from a deficiency of the vital fluid. For the most part, however, the scientific community reacted with dismay and disbelief, even though the basic principles of endocrinology, including the role of sex hormones, were rather well understood. In fact, Brown-Séquard's predecessor at the Collège de France was Claude Bernard, the physiologist credited with originating the expression "internal secretion" and with initiating the study of the endocrine glands and their hormones.

Among the critics of Brown-Séquard's work was the journal *Wiener Medizinische Wochenschrift*, which offered a comment typical of the many the French scientists had to endure: "Professor Brown-Séquard's audience appears to have received an impression of the intellectual capacity of the aged scientist very different from that which he, in his elevated frame of mind, evidently expected to produce. The lecture must be regarded as further proof of the necessity of retiring professors who have attained their threescore and ten." The *Boston Medical and Surgical Journal* warned loftily: "The sooner the general public and especially septuagenarian readers of the latest sensation understand that for the physically used up and worn out there is no secret of rejuvenation, no elixir of youth, the better." Others regarded Brown-Séquard's claim as a case of autosuggestion and put it aside, or they speculated that an erotic rather than a vivifying effect had been his aim all along.

An unfortunate result of Brown-Séquard's experiments, aside from the disappointment it brought to elderly males sold on rejuvenation at a magic fountain of sperm, was the restriction it placed on the burgeoning science of endocrinology. It was some time before the reaction to his experiments and the constraints this placed on hormone studies wore away enough to permit a continuation of the important, albeit more intuitive than critical, research he began. Most endocrinologists would agree today that Brown-Séquard's method of extracting male hormone from animal testicles was too crude to produce quantities sufficient to bring about the results he claimed. For one thing, the male hormone is produced in the testes and sent out into the bloodstream; it is not stored in the glands, ready to be tapped like some precious well of oil. The Frenchman also put too much emphasis on what the testicles produced, concluding erroneously that sexual potency and rejuvenated bodily functions — he even claimed that his bowel movements were better after the injections — were closely linked. A case he was fond of citing involved two men, one forty-five the other fifty. "At my advice, each time they had a great piece of work, either physical or intellectual, to accomplish, they put themselves into a state of active sexual excitement, avoiding, however, all seminal ejaculation. The glands of the testicles then temporarily acquired great functional activity, which was soon followed by the desired augmentation of power in the nervous centers."

What, then, did account for Brown-Séquard's "rejuvenation"? The best answer, in light of today's medical knowledge, is that the injections he gave himself acted as a placebo, an inactive substance given as a medication to humor a patient and which might possibly work some positive psychogenic effect. The traces of hormone that may have slipped through the aging scientist's skin were considerably less powerful than his will to restore himself sexually, mentally and physically.

The chauvinistic notion that the secret to long life lay dormant in the gonads — none of the early rejuvenators appears to have bothered to make the same connection to the female ovaries — did not, unfortunately, die with Brown-Séquard. His injection therapy, radical as it was by the day's standards, was benign in comparison to what followed. There was, for one, Eugen Steinach (1861–1944), an Austrian physiologist and director of the Biological Institute of the Academy of Sciences in Vienna. Convinced that Brown-Séquard's intuitions about internal secretions were correct, Steinach performed a series of experiments with rats in which he severed their sperm ducts on the theory that the backup of spermatozoa would force more hormones into the blood. These tests led to his vasoligature operation, which involved tying off the vas deferens, the tube that carries sperm from the testicles to the glands where they are stored just before ejaculation. Today, the operation is referred to as a vasectomy and entails cutting the vas. When this is accomplished on both sides, the male becomes sterile but retains his potency. Steinach's aim, however, was to rejuvenate, not to control conception.

On November 1, 1918, Dr. Robert Lichtenstern, a

Viennese urologist who had watched Steinach's laboratory experiments, performed the first vasoligature on a
human, the aim being to restore the patient's vitality.
The subject, Anton W., was forty-three years old, 108
pounds, "not old in years but prematurely senile and ex-
hausted." The operation, according to all accounts, was a
success. Three months later, Anton W.'s appetite was
described as excellent, his appearance as hale, his skin
texture smoother and his weight markedly increased. In
a year, his physical condition was described as "splen-
did," his muscle development "extraordinary." Many
years after, in a review of the work, Steinach com-
mented, "This, therefore, was the first case, the signal for
a new hormone therapy, which proved itself in the
course of the following two decades in many thousands,
perhaps even tens of thousands, of successful operations." The process of aging, he believed, could be influenced. But, again, whether his operation released an
overabundance of hormones to do that is doubtful, and
references to his work, when they can be found at all, are
sketchy. In its table of methods section, *Stedman's Medical Dictionary* refers to the operation simply as "a subcutaneous division of the vas deferens, which is claimed
to cause a rejuvenation of elderly men." In any event, the
matter is immaterial today because of the synthesis of
male hormone, the potential of which Steinach himself
foresaw: "Today, we may disregard the initial opposition
to vasoligature. Reactivation by means of accumulation
of natural testicular hormone has long since secured itself a place in clinical medicine. And if there is anything
that could possibly dislodge it from that place, it could

be only reactivation by means of artificial sex hormones, which rests upon the basis of and imitates natural hormone therapy."

Steinach's work, like Brown-Séquard's, stirred controversy that was fed through no fault of Steinach by the sensational press. Few took his experiments seriously, and most of his colleagues regarded him, at best, as a misguided eccentric. Denied a visa to the United States, where he wished to pursue and refine his work, Steinach died bitter and depressed in Swiss exile, his vasoligature ridiculed by the scientific community and forgotten, except in its file drawers, by a fickle press. But he was, in all fairness, a meticulous scientist who, I suspect, did not seek out the wave of publicity that kept his experiments in the public notice. He was generally restrained about his work and rarely discussed it outside of his dwindling circle of friends.

Not so the wealthy, urbane Serge Voronoff, a Russian-born charmer and surgeon who moved to France in the late 1800s and soon thereafter became as adept at self-promotion as he was with his scalpel. His name first appears on the roster of rejuvenators in connection with his observations of eunuchs, those castrated Eastern harem attendants who, like other unsexed animal species, are plumpish and show signs of premature aging.

"The caponized cock's comb withers away and the bird ceases to crow," Voronoff declared. "It loses at the same time its fighting spirit, its courage, its instincts for domination and for protecting its hens." He made much of the castrated bull transformed into an ox and placidly drawing a wagon driven by a child, and he talked often of the diminishing effect castration has on the bony framework and the flesh of animals. It was during a stay in Egypt that Voronoff examined a number of middle-aged eunuchs and found them to have imperfectly developed muscles, an absence of bodily hair (except on the scalp), decreased organic function, wrinkled and scaly skin, white hair, and signs of *arcus senilis,* an opaque ring around the iris that usually appears about age seventy. They were also lacking in physical strength, were indolent and languid, anemic and prone to infection. "Well before death, they have the appearance of old men," Voronoff observed, "and from this one might be tempted to attribute a very advanced age to them. But this would be pure illusion. They have every appearance of being effectively aged: dry skin, bloated body, dull eyes. They have a stopping gait which gives one the impression that they are centenarians." Decrepit old men, Voronoff noted, are really eunuchs emasculated "not by the criminal hand of man but by the cruel law of nature, by the wear and tear of old age." When the genital glands cease to function, he added, when amorous ardor is lost, the elderly become as eunuchs. On the other hand, if the male genitals remain vigorous and produce their external and internal secretions freely and abundantly, then youth is prolonged far beyond the usual duration. Said Voronoff: "Men thus fortunately endowed reach advanced ages. Possession of active genital glands constitutes the best possible assurance of long life."

Soon after World War I, he decided to test that idea. "Now we have learned what a wonderful source of youth Nature has placed in our glands," he said. "The veil is lifted from our brains and we must have the daring, now that this knowledge has been acquired, and this secret revealed, to force Nature to keep us young until the supreme moment when we must fade away."

He chose an unconventional way to accomplish this: transplanting bits and pieces of apes' testes into elderly men. Grafting had actually been attempted earlier by the aforementioned Lichtenstern, who in 1915, performed the operation on a young soldier who had lost both testicles in a gunshot accident. Two months after he suffered the wound, the youth developed all the typical signs of a castrate: extra weight, disappearance of facial hair and mustache, and emotional upset, especially about sex. It happened that another soldier was in the same military hospital for correction of an undescended testicle and a strangulated inguinal hernia. One of his testicles was removed, cut in half, and each half sutured into a pocket in the wounded soldier's abdomen. A fortnight later, the soldier was well and, according to one account, enjoying erotic dreams. With time, the patient lost his extra adipose tissue; his pubic hair and mustache returned and, said his surgeon, he had no more complaints about his sex life (though he was sterile). Twenty years later, he was reported to have a normal masculine appearance, normal intelligence, and was happily married.

But before he attempted to duplicate these results in aging males, Voronoff tried another operation — transplanting the thyroid gland of a chimpanzee into the neck of a fifteen-year-old boy suffering from cretinism. This severe thyroid deficiency had made the youth backward, indolent and apathetic. "Verging on the animal state" was the way Voronoff described such children. The surgeon watched the boy closely for fourteen months and noticed a gradual improvement. He resumed growing, and his face, which had taken on a yellow hue — and his nose and lips, which had become swollen — returned to normal. The apathy and drowsiness disappeared, and the child became more active, finally returning to school. Several years later, Voronoff received a letter from the boy's father who begged the surgeon to use his Paris contacts to secure for his son a less hazardous station than the one he had been assigned in the front line trenches. Said Voronoff proudly: "Thus, little Jean, whom I had known in 1912 as a poor little imbecile, with a rudimentary brain and the body of an eight-year-old child, had been declared four years later fit for military service and had marched off to defend his country like any other man."

Voronoff's attempt to restore youth began with animals, notably with his Ram No. 14, twelve years old, the equivalent of ninety in a human, trembling limbs, incontinent, wool thin and bald in places, and in general, in a most pitiable state. In the spring of 1918, Voronoff grafted the animal with the genitals from a two-year-old lamb, and three months later Ram No. 14 was transformed. His wool was thicker, the trembling was gone, the warlike behavior returned, the sexual instincts were evident. A year later, Voronoff removed the grafts and watched as the old animal began to go downhill again. He did a second graft, and the animal's vigor returned, lasting for three years. A third graft was performed with comparable results, including the return of full powers of procreation. Six days before it finally died, Ram No. 14 suddenly declined, lost his appetite, and became drowsy. "Its old age lasted six days," Voronoff reported, "instead of five years, in spite of the fact that it had exceeded by six years the life of the longest-lived individual of its race. The case of this ram indicates to us the course to be pursued, the ideal to be attained: the prolongation of the length of life and the shortening of the period of old age, thanks to gland-grafting." He added smugly that autosuggestion, which some of his colleagues invoked when criticizing similar results obtained in humans, would obviously be put aside in this case.

Elated by the experience with Ram No. 14, Voronoff turned his attention to elderly males, planning at first to use the gonads of young, robust human volunteer donors to rejuvenate his aging patients. Few, however, came forward, and those who did offer their precious testicles placed too high a dollar value on them, even for a man of Voronoff's means. So he turned to the next best thing — apes of all sizes and sorts. Eventually, he performed over 2,000 grafts of sex glands from higher species of monkeys, suturing them securely into place in his human patients. His fees were high and the newspaper coverage was spectacular. There was, for one, the case of E. L., grafted with a monkey's testicles at the age of seventy-four, heavy, bent, sunken features and dull eyes, who walked with difficulty, leaning on a stick, impotent for twelve years. Eight months after the transplant, Voronoff

professed to be "literally stupefied" when E. L. dropped
by. He was, according to the surgeon, jovial, his eyes
were clear and twinkling with amusement at the aston-
ishment displayed by Voronoff and his clinical assistant.
Most of his obesity had disappeared, his muscles appeared firmer, and he walked erect. "He bent his head
and revealed to our astonished eyes a growth of white
down," said Voronoff. "Formerly, there had been a bald
expanse. He came to see us from Switzerland where he
had been climbing and taking part in various sports so
favored by Englishmen. The man was literally 15 to 20
years younger; the graft had transferred a senile, impotent, pitiful old being into a vigorous man in full possession of all his faculties."

Although he concentrated on restoring men, a few of
his patients were women. One was a forty-eight-year-old
Brazilian who came to the surgeon for a graft because
her husband had left her. She had become too old to
please him, she said. Voronoff described her as very fat
and looking all of her age, perhaps more. "It at once
occurred to me that grafting might have great influence
in this case since it might reunite the sacred bonds of the
family and enable this woman to regain her unkind husband by means of charms recovered and graces renewed
and freshened." Voronoff grafted her with a female monkey's sex glands, and four months later reported her
"formless body converted into a charming personality."
Two years later, when he saw her again, she looked
thirty-five. Asked whether her marital happiness had
been restored as well, she replied with a coy smile, "I did

not go back to my husband. He was not worthy of me."
Voronoff, like Steinach, ended up unhonored and un-
sung, stunned by the realization, according to one account, that not only were many of his testicular grafts
being rejected — remember that this was long before the
days of kidney transplants and immunosuppressive drugs
that prevent rejection — but the recipients had been in-
fected with syphilis from the monkey donors. He died in
obscurity.

Today, transplantation of gonads or ovaries is not a
treatment for aging or little else for that matter, simply
because the hormones secreted by those glands — estrogen in the female, androgen in the male — can be supplied in pill or injection form. Dr. Francis D. Moore,
professor of surgery at Harvard Medical School and one
of the world's leading authorities on transplantation,
points out that some young women are born with ovaries
that do not grow or mature normally. In these women an
ovarian transplant, even if it did not make for the release
of eggs for reproductive purposes, could make for a more
normal life. In males, a similar condition is called
eunuchoidism, and though it is rare, according to Dr.
Moore, here again transplantation of testicular tissue
would have significance. But to believe that there could
possibly be any rejuvenating effect, or any halting of the
cellular changes that come with senility, through the
Voronoff operation is rather absurd. Any passage of
hormonal material to the aging recipient would be a passive transfer — that is, it would have but transient
eroticizing effects, lasting only a few days. Moreover, to
surgically join the tiny vessels that feed ovaries and tes-

ticles is no mean task, even with today's refined transplant methods. A microscope is often used to do the job right, and a suturing machine, a device that sends staples of microscopic size into the blood vessel walls, is essential. Voronoff's testicular connection was a tenuous one, to say the least.

Part II

Rejuvenation

Introduction

SCIENCE, GERONTOLOGY INCLUDED, operates in a unique intellectual, social and political climate. The vast bulk of its practitioners are faceless benchworkers in white lab coats, people who perform endlessly repetitive analyses in beakers and under microscopes and on paper, jotting down the results in green-covered notebooks or feeding them into computer storage from which they will eventually emerge on a chattering printout, summoned by some chief scientist who needs the data to buttress his or her own theories or knock down that of another.

There are, really, two kinds of science which these people practice, and much has been written about the difference between them. They are known as "basic" and "applied," but while they have different objectives each is no more or no less important than the other, nor are the scientists themselves accorded any special place in the academic pecking order. Basic research in aging is geared to learning more about fundamental biological events and seeks to accumulate a store of knowledge from which the practical applications of the science may be spun out.

There is, of course, great potential for mitigating aging's effects and even for slowing its progress in each and every one of the current ideas about its causes —

disease, repeated exposure to physical and mental stress, chemical reactions that cause natural decay, radiation, temperature, the body's disease-fighting immune system gone awry, accumulation of "age pigments," intermolecular cross-linking, diet, inadequate oxygen in the lungs and blood, malfunctions in the genetic program that cause protein synthesis errors, and finally, in the notion that pacemakers of aging, located either in each one of the body's cells or in some central place in the brain, are behind it all.

In the last analysis, the proof of the many theories of aging's causes is found in the successful, practical application of what the basic scientists preach. But, given our current allotted life spans and the predictions of our insurance company statisticians that those spans are not likely to change dramatically for some time to come, it should be obvious that there are far more theories than there are valid therapies for aging. The labors of the aforementioned rejuvenators produced minimal and questionable results, and some of the approaches being suggested today might not pan out for generations. In this section, we will examine a few of the more practical attempts to slow down or assuage aging. Some are promising, although confined for the moment to animal tests. Others, according to those who administer or partake of them, actually work.

Whether the natural course of aging is irreversible is not yet known. What is certain, though, is that medical science may well have reached the limit of its ability to add to the human life span by a conventional, disease-oriented approach. Imagine, if you will, that the world has been transformed through the brilliance and persistence of science into a healthy Utopia, a place, truly, of better living through chemistry. All the major diseases that killed us off in the past are gone for good — no more cancer, no more heart disease, no more stroke. Because of the absence of lethal illness, we might conclude that in this ideal world we would all be endowed with markedly longer and more vigorous lives, maybe not exactly Methuselahs leaping tall buildings in single bounds but, still, lasting longer than our ancestors. It is true that with the conquest of such life-threatening childhood diseases as diphtheria and bacterial pneumonia, and the control of polio, typhoid and smallpox, more people survive into their sixties and seventies. When humans first began to record history, they could expect to live about twenty years. Today, with improved medical care, better sanitation and proper nutrition, a child born in America can expect to live to around seventy, more than a score of years longer than it could have at the turn of the century. More and more of us are reaching the upper age brackets. That the aged constitute a greater proportion of the country's population is attested to by statistics showing that some ten percent of all Americans today are sixty-five or older, compared to four percent in 1900. Furthermore, according to some estimates, with the coming to retirement of the offspring of the postwar baby boom, somewhere around the year 2000, the sixty-five-plus population will make up a quarter of us all.

But impressive as this seems, life expectancy has remained at around seventy years since 1955. And though it is tempting to assume that longevity will take a quantum leap if the diseases and stresses that plague us were eliminated, such is not the case. For even if we managed to escape accident, disease or the hand of an enemy, we would probably still be dead by one hundred. Even if there were a cure for all forms of cancer, or if the disease could be prevented, we would add but two years to our life span. The experts also tell us that if we add in a cure for heart disease and all the primary diseases, we'd probably buy about twenty or so years in all. What it amounts to is that we would be able to live our lives out — an allotted span — in a healthier condition, free of the threat of *premature* death, not free of the fear of death itself. Death, then, is more a function of that thing we call age than of any specific disease process. It is age that kills us all in the end, if all goes on schedule, and not some disease.

Chapter Three

CONSIDER FOR A MOMENT the lowly salamander, whose name was given in ancient times to a mythical lizard purportedly able to live in fire because of the chill of its body. Indeed, Paracelsus saw it as the elemental being of fire, purifier of all the impure metals. As we know it today, the salamander is a tailed amphibian, a newt, with a smooth, moist skin that inhabits water in the tadpole state, returning to the water only to deposit its eggs. Generally it prefers damp and humid dwelling places under stones, in rotted stumps or in the roots of a tree. Its food consists of slugs, insects and worms, and according to those who study it, it is shy, sluggish and quite stupid.

What, you might well ask, has this ignoble creature to do with gerontology and rejuvenation? A good deal, as it turns out. For salamanders (along with crabs) are able to do something that scientists investigating the formation, structure and breakdown of tissues wish we could do — they can grow new limbs when their old ones are amputated. So, too, can the hydra, a remarkable multicellular freshwater animal. Its powers of regeneration are even more incredible. Chopped into fairly large pieces, each piece develops into a complete new organism; small bits of hydra, when placed close together, reform into another hydra. Human beings, on the other hand, can regenerate only hair, skin, nails, bone and part of the liver.

We have difficulty with structures involving multiple kinds of tissue, and although we can scar these structures over with connective tissues we cannot regenerate them. Just why this is the case has puzzled scientists for generations. Among the first to ask the question was Lazzaro Spallanzani, discoverer of the digestive properties of saliva and a pioneer in regeneration studies. In 1768, he posed this problem: "If frogs are able to renew their legs when young, why should they not do the same when farther advanced? Are the wonderful reproductions mentioned in the newts only to be ascribed to the effect of water, in which these animals were kept? This is contradicted in the instance of the salamander, whose parts were reproduced even on dry ground. But if the above-mentioned animals, either aquatic or amphibian, recover their legs when kept on dry ground, how comes it to pass that other land animals, such as are accounted perfect, and are better known to us, are not endowed with the same power? Is it to be hoped that they may acquire them by some useful dispositions?"

Armed with the answer to the regeneration question, researchers might well be on their way to a better understanding of disease processes, and to fulfilling a prediction made a few years ago by Dr. James Bonner, of the California Institute of Technology, that if a cell's genetic program could be reset, we might be able to prolong life by encouraging a cell or group of cells to turn into a new organ. A cell with its inner workings programmed for, say, a heart or kidney, might be cultured in a laboratory hothouse, then reimplanted in two or three years when the new organ is fully grown and the old one shows signs of failing. Rejection, the problem that bedevils organ transplants, would not occur since the cells from which the new tissue was grown were not foreign to the recipient. Theoretically at least, one could replace any defective organ simply by growing a new one when the time came because every organ seems to have the potential for regrowth built into it. What is lacking at the present is a proper trigger. But scientists know that under certain conditions the body compensates for the loss of an organ by causing other parts of the body to assume enlarged functions. Researchers at burns institutes use that knowledge in their search for factors that cause this sort of natural activity, as well as the means by which it might be artificially induced. The hope is that one day it will be possible to regenerate a new hand instead of tediously repairing one that has been, say, severely burned. Scientists have already made some progress in replacing defective body parts through the use of transplants and artificial organs. And there have been startling successes and abysmal failures in grafts involving hearts, kidneys, parathyroid glands, lungs, ovaries, larynxes, spleens, skin, corneas, livers and bone marrow.

In addition, today's transplanters have even taken a cue from Voronoff, and in 1963 and 1964 demonstrated that chimpanzee kidneys could function in a human being, thereby giving rise to the currently held belief that xenografting — transplanting animal organs to humans — may be a reality in the near future. The wider availability of animal organs removes the logistic limitation, and their use eliminates some of the ethical and legal problems as well. Scientists are also giving thought to the development of artificial organs driven by air, or electric or atomic power. Recent reports, in fact, note that survival time with a totally artificial heart in experimental animals is some 1,500 times greater than it was years ago. In 1958, for example, survival time with such a heart was ninety minutes; in 1974 it reached ninety-four days. Says artificial organ expert Willem Kolff of the Cleveland Clinic: "The irreparably sick human heart will be replaced in the near future by a mechanical pump. Although I have been told that nobody will want such a machine inside his chest, I think that the person who said this did not realize that for a person who really needs it, the alternative is not popular either."

But grafting whole organs and implanting artificial ones, while they are exciting possibilities for longevity researchers, are by their very nature stopgap measures that could easily be rendered individually ineffective if another vital organ or system that has not or cannot be replaced gives way. An artificial heart would not add any extra years to the patient dying of liver cancer unless the cancer could be wiped out and the liver regrown also. A similar equalizing effect would hold true with organ grafts. It is, then, highly unlikely that any of us will witness, or our children's children witness, bicentennarian human beings functioning normally, loaded with all the extras that biomedical engineering can fabricate from plastic or borrow from chimp or fellow human being. There is simply too broad a constellation of difficulties — rejection, availability and preservation of organs, infection, finding the proper material for constructing artificial viscera. There are the host of ethical and legal issues: rights of the organ donor, especially if he or she is retarded; determining whether a transplant treatment is worse than the disease; proper definition of death, an important consideration when a transplanter is about to remove an organ for grafting; the question of who receives an organ from a bank, and who makes the decision to allocate.

All of which makes organ regeneration extremely attractive to researchers eager to duplicate in humans the ability certain animals have to regrow vital parts. If we could stimulate our bodies to do this naturally, there is no telling how many extra years we might buy. As we said earlier, we already have limited capacity to do it — skin, hair, nails and portions of the liver can be regrown. The last — the body's largest glandular organ with an array of functions ranging from storing vitamins to purifying the blood — presents researchers with probably their strongest argument for human organ regeneration. For years, we have known that when as much as eighty or even ninety percent of the liver is surgically removed from experimental animals, virtually the entire organ will regenerate. This remarkable process occurs also in humans, often with amazing speed, so long as the small amount of liver left after resection has an adequate blood supply. A few years ago, Dr. Jan K. Siemsen, a radiologist at the University of Southern California, ran radioisotope scans on a number of patients at Los Angeles County–USC Medical Center. The patients had had large portions of their livers removed. All regrew a normal-sized functioning liver — and in one case the organ regenerated in a week. Interestingly, the larger the portion of liver removed, the quicker the organ regrew; in some cases where a smaller portion was cut out, it did not regrow. Furthermore, the organ regenerated no matter which area of it was removed, and it did so without any outside means of stimulation. The process simply occurred as a natural bodily function.

The reason resected livers regenerate has been under investigation for some time, and while the issue is not yet settled, all available evidence points toward a hormone present in the circulatory system that supplies the abdominal organs. This "regenerating factor" has yet to be isolated, but if and when it is, clinicians of the future may be using it to treat such disorders as cirrhosis, a chronic disease in which active liver cells are blotted out by inactive scar tissue. Though we may never be able to overdrink with impunity, it is somewhat comforting to know that our livers, at least, may one day be protected.

Other scientists have turned their attention to regrowing bones. At Columbia University Hospital, for instance, a new electromagnetic technique has been developed that successfully promotes bone regeneration in children with congenital pseudoarthrosis, an affliction also known as "false joint," that is the result of failure of fractured bone ends to unite. For several years before, scientists had some degree of success healing bone fractures by implanting electrodes in the bone near the fracture site, then turning on an electrical current. Dr. Andrew Bassett of Columbia was able to regenerate bone in five children *without* electrode implantation. A cast is first applied to the limb, then a pair of coils is inserted into it on either side of the break. When pulsed with 24 to 30 volts, the coils supply a magnetic field at right angles to the bone which induces a voltage near the fracture site. In all five children, there was good union of the fracture, and there were no recurrences of the disease. Even though the healing mechanism of electromagnetic action is unclear, researchers believe the technique may ultimately be applied to routine fractures and may cut healing time by as much as fifty percent.

Although all of these attempts at regenerating and transplanting whole body parts are promising and may well give us all a new lease on life some day, more than likely any startling successes will come not on the whole organ level first, but on the cellular. Working in that area, scientists at the University of Chicago recently isolated, grew, and replicated human heart cells, duplicating earlier work in rats. Up to this point, all the existing evidence indicated that human, rat or chicken muscle cells stop dividing soon after birth and fail to regenerate new muscle after injury in the adult. A team led by Dr. Donald A. Fischman established cultures of heart muscle cells and watched them send out branches similar to the protrusions amoebas employ to move about and engulf their food. While these muscle cell extensions appeared to lack the machinery necessary to make them contract — as do viable heart muscle cells — they did contain the nucleus and other cellular organelles needed for life. The results of this experiment must be interpreted cautiously, but they do suggest fairly strongly that the muscle damage that occurs after a coronary may not necessarily be irreversible. And though the work is still preliminary, it could conceivably lead to improved methods for regrowing heart muscle after attack or surgery, and in the establishment of heart cell banks from which surgeons could draw healthy muscle to replace dead or scarred tissue. Drawing on stores of rejuvenating cellular material is not as farfetched as it sounds. In fact, it is being done throughout the world in centers that offer a controversial form of cell transplantation known as CT, for cellular therapy. Originated in 1931 by the Swiss surgeon and glandular expert Paul Niehans, CT is probably the most commercially successful of all the attempts to wipe away the ravages of age. That year, another physician referred a woman to Niehans for a parathyroid graft, hoping that it would cure her of a severe case of tetany. This is a convulsive disorder caused by insufficient calcium in the blood and is often associated with disease of the parathyroid glands. Because the patient was dying, a transplant was out of the question, so Niehans did the next best thing — he minced the parathyroids of an ox, mixed them into a solution, and injected the liquid into the woman's pectoral muscles. "I thought the effect would be short-lived, just like the effect of an injection of hormones," Niehans wrote later, "and that I should have to repeat the injection. But to my great surprise, the injection of fresh cells not only failed to provoke a reaction but the effect lasted, and longer than any synthetic hormone, any implant or any surgical graft." Twenty-five years later, the woman was still free of the disease's cramps, which so pleased Niehans that he exulted, "Implantation of organs surgically gave way to implantation of organs by injection, which is fundamentally a thousandfold injection."

Practicing on himself, on patients and on animals, Niehans injected solutions made from the cells of just about every organ he could obtain from fetal animals. Sheep were preferred because of their generally good health, resistance to disease, and the rarity of allergic reactions after their protein is used therapeutically. The various organs used were collected under scrupulously sterile conditions. A private abattoir supplied the pregnant ewes, who were knocked unconscious, opened surgically, and their uteruses drawn out, detached, wrapped in sterile drapes, and taken to a laboratory where they were cut open and the organs of the fetuses extracted.

Niehans's injection therapy was specific: a fetal heart muscle for damaged human heart muscle, for circulatory problems and for undersized hearts; liver cells for anemia, cirrhosis and insufficient blood corpuscles; cells from fetal gastric mucosa for treating diminished gastric juices; kidney cells for nephritis; spleen cells for muscular weakness and iron deficiency anemia; hypothalamic cells for asthma. The thymus he viewed as "the gland of youth," injecting its extract in cases of dwarfism, exhaustion after long illness and mongolism.

Placenta cells he injected to treat undeveloped breasts and exhaustion after difficult childbirth, reasoning that many animals eat the afterbirth "and in that way recover astonishing strength." But it was the sex glands which Niehans saw as concealing incalculable riches. In one Voronovian surge, he exclaimed, "The sex glands are not merely glands where spermatozoa and ova are formed; their internal secretions are a rich source of vital fluids which give physical strength, intellectual freshness and also physical qualities. They also revitalize the aging organism. Even the mind and soul of a genius need these precious secretions. Between birth and death, puberty and the climacteric are the most critical times in our lives. The hidden forces of the sex glands lead us from the unconscious paradise of childhood to the sparkling life of youth, to the strength of the fully-grown man; with their gradual drying up, old age begins." Consequently, he administered injections of male testicular cells for a long list of problems: diminished libido, impotence, chain-smoking, undeveloped and malfunctioning testicles, homosexuality, "sexual neuroses," throbbing headaches, insomnia, acne and eczema and itching anus, undernourishment, depression, and "as a curative measure in cancer of the prostate" as well as a "prophylactic against the development of cancer in the man."

Indications for injections of female sex glands were just as general: menopausal difficulties, ovarian disturbances, lesbian tendencies, sterility of ovarian origin, hirsutism, itching vulva, inferiority complex, signs of premature aging, and as a cancer prophylaxis. "What I am striving after," Niehans explained, "is not only to give more years to life, but especially to give more life to years."

A single treatment, according to Niehans, was often enough to do the job because each injection was equivalent to the transplantation of the organ multiplied a thousand times, and because the cells, on account of the extent of their surfaces, could easily be provided with oxygen and the "nutritive lymph of the organism." Thus, Niehans believed, the curative effects are not only amazingly good but generally lasting.

Deaths and widespread infections have occurred after CT practiced by unskilled and careless opportunists, but Niehans's record, and that of others of his caliber, is favorable. In fact, he claimed more than 50,000 injections without losing a patient, and treated himself with testicular cells for a prostate condition. His eight cardinal rules dictated serological examination of the animals to screen out disease, thorough examination of the patients, no injections in the presence of infection, abattoirs in the immediate vicinity of his clinic (Clinique La Prairie at Clarens on Lake Geneva), fresh cells (frozen or dried cells are used by other clinics today), absolute mastery of the technique, bed rest for several days, withholding all other remedies such as hormones and vaccines. "I never take anyone into the clinic without a doctor's certificate," Niehans told one interviewer, "to protect my place as a doctor." Today, patients check in at nearby hotels on a Sunday and undergo a couple of days of testing before receiving the injections. One of the tests is the questionable Abderhalden Reaction, once used to determine pregnancy, malignant disease, goiter, schizophrenia, and other conditions. Supposedly able to determine the presence of protective ferments — organic catalysts that produce fermentation — in the blood, the test produces varied results and is not widely used. But, according to Niehans, it indicates with absolute certainty which organs lack cells. Patients are kept in bed for a day or so after their injections and must remain at the clinic for another week or more as a precaution. While there, they receive these directions: "Your organism has been given precious cells, which start to work after three and a half months. I beg you not to damage them in any way! Therefore, no x-rays without protecting the rest of the body, no short-wave treatment, no ultraviolet rays, no very hot hair dryer, no bath cures in radioactive thermal stations, no sunbaths, no Turkish baths, no sauna baths, no diathermy, no poisons such as nicotine, concentrated alcohol, no drugs (if possible), no hormones. These instructions are for your whole life long."

Thousands seeking to regain their youth and vitality have flocked to the clinique or to Niehans's many disciples who have set up shop in Germany, London, and in a few other parts of the world, and received injections of cells of unborn lambs into the muscles of their buttocks or thighs. Niehans died in 1971 at the age of eighty-nine,

leaving a lucrative enterprise and a grand roster of re-
vitalized former patients, their tired old cells reportedly
regenerated by the doses of fresh fetal cells — names including Konrad Adenauer, W. Somerset Maugham, Char-
lie Chaplin, Bernard Baruch, Charles De Gaulle. With
customers like these as testimonials, with a Voronoff-like
genius for publicity and promotion, and with a truly dis-
tinguished background (a Hohenzollern with a doc-
torate in theology, decorated for World War I bravery
by the King of Serbia, an accomplished horseman and
marksman, and vast experience as a surgeon, diagnosti-
cian and endocrinologist), Niehans built CT into the
elixir vitae most sought after in this century.

But, despite its popularity, cellular therapy is not
ordinarily practiced in the ghetto, and the perennial
quest for pristine vigor via organ injection is pretty
much limited by the size of the checkbook. CT patients
are invariably moneyed actors, actresses and elder
statesmen who seclude themselves in luxurious villas
near the clinic. Probably the best publicity CT ever got
was its use to treat an ailing Pius XII in 1954. The pope
was suffering from a gastric disorder never clearly described and his doctors called in Niehans. One of the
other physicians on the Holy Father's case, incidentally,
was Professor Galeazzi-Lisi who wound up in difficulty
with Italian organized medicine for selling photographs
and a report of Pius's last hours. Niehans, according to
one account, gave the seventy-seven-year-old pope injections of freeze-dried cells because he couldn't bring
sheep into the Vatican, and restored his strength. Later
the same year, Pius was plagued by a strangulated

diaphragmatic hernia; called in again, Niehans advised against surgery, but this time got His Holiness's stomach back in shape with a diet of mashed potatoes and potato soup. Administering cell therapy is one thing, but trying to determine and explain how it actually works is another. Niehans himself was unsure of the mechanism, remarking on more than one occasion: "I am no scientist." His standard explanation was that cellular therapy was a method of "treating the whole organism on a biological basis, capable of revitalizing it with its trillions of cells by bringing to it those embryonic or young cells which it needs." The statement smacks a little of Brown-Séquard and Voronoff, and is too general to satisfy any scientist-critic of Niehans's work. But Niehans did not usually write for scientists, a fact that forms the basis of much of the criticism of him by the medical establishment. It should be noted here also that the establishment took a dim view of his press agentry and high fees. He was convinced, however, if we can believe his statements, that CT did work and that was all that mattered. The rationale for such treatment, he was fond of pointing out, was rooted in ancient medicine that taught the organs of young animals had a strengthening and curative effect. Indeed, the oldest medical document known, the Papyrus of Eber, mentions preparations produced from animal organs. Skin transplants from animals to man were suggested by Hippocrates; the Hindus, a thousand years before Christ, believed that eating sex glands of tigers cured impotency; Homer mentions that Achilles ate the bone marrow of lions to bolster his strength and courage; and in the third century, Chinese physicians prescribed human placenta as a tonic.

Niehans also relied heavily on the experiments of others with chicken heart fragments — particularly Alexis Carrel's observations that dying cell cultures may be rejuvenated by the addition of similar fresh cells — to support his therapy. And to further buttress his contention that an underfunctioning human organ is best treated by the cells of the same organ of the animal, he liked to quote Paracelsus: "The heart heals the heart, kidney heals kidney, spleen heals spleen, *similia similibus curantur*. Like heals like."

Many people have undoubtedly been helped by CT, but whether the injections act as vaccination with organ-specific effects, as a crude hormone treatment, or simply have some placebo effect is not yet known. It has also been suggested that some cell therapists are merely Dr. Feelgoods making a financial killing by inoculating slipping jet-setters with cellular extracts laced with amphetamines, hormones and vitamins. Among those not impressed was the American Medical Association's Department of Investigation, which reported in 1960 that the most one could say for CT was that it was experimental at best. The AMA also took issue with the methods used to promote the therapy and accused those who practice it of creating a demand for it simply because they cannot swerve critical observers to their side. On the other hand, the AMA called attention to an earlier report on *The Treatment of Mental Deficiency and*

Encephalopathies in Childhood by Means of Fresh Tissue and Siccacell, which appeared in the *Archives of Pediatrics.* (Siccacell is the trade name for freeze-dried cells produced by a German firm set up by Niehans.) The report described a treatment in a Berlin hospital in which a section of calf brain was stirred into a mash with penicillin and injected into the buttocks of young mentally retarded patients and others with cerebral palsy and pituitary insufficiency. Following the treatment, according to the report, the children became more alert and balanced, had better appetites, slept more restfully. They also took a more active part in the daily life of the family, showed more interest in schoolwork, improved in memory and intelligence, and even physically grew more in cases where the injection was made prior to puberty. In children with mongolism, the treatment steadied the ungainly, uncertain and straddle-legged gait so typical of the disorder.

This sort of treatment is not available in the United States, however, since the Food and Drug Administration has frowned on importing the materials used in cell therapy. Still, the antidrug, "natural" aspects of CT appeal to many, much as do acupuncture and chiropractic, and like those two techniques CT offers consumers an opportunity to test the validity of organized medicine's often haughty disregard for any medical practice that is foreign-based, popular or practiced by non-physicians. So, along with the princely types who flock to the Lake Geneva clinic can be found an occasional middle American who feels it all might be worth the budgeting he or she has done for a treatment in London — plus air fare and accommodations — that is part of a vacation package.

Cellular therapy, thus far, has not become part of medicine's mainstream, although it has sent its practitioners smiling to the bank. The customers also seem pleased with the results. There may be just enough science involved to keep it from being entirely dismissed, and it may well be that CT is not a fad or fraud, as some charge, but an immunological puzzle that could lead to other forms of treatment for aging or for the diseases that accompany it. Some scientists have told me privately that they believe the biological answer to what makes CT appear to work may be found in research now under way in immunotherapy, that branch of science which attempts to shore up the body's natural defenses against disease. For instance, infusions of infection-fighting white blood cells to strengthen a failing immune system and bone marrow transplants to combat leukemia and aplastic anemia are, despite some formidable obstacles blocking their routine use, very much a part of twentieth-century medicine's mixed bag of therapies. Scientists know, too, that some cells may be capable of living much longer than the whole organism which they make up. At the Jackson Laboratory in Bar Harbor, Maine, one project has, in fact, already demonstrated that marrow cell lines transplanted from old mice to younger ones can continue to function normally for a period of time equal to two-and-a-half times the life span of the mouse that donated the marrow cells. Researchers are also interested in the cells in the pancreas, which secretes insulin. These cells are called the islets of Langerhans. Rather than graft a new pancreas, with all of the difficulties that entails, into a diabetic, scientists have proposed (and succeeded in monkeys) harvesting vast quantities of islets from human donors and injecting them into those suffering from the disease. (There have been only some forty pancreas transplants worldwide at this writing, compared with thousands of kidney grafts, and only five have survived over ten months, with one alive two-and-a-half years after operation. First year survival rate of kidney grafts from cadaver organs is seventy-two percent.) One estimate is that ten to twenty percent of the million islets in the human pancreas would be necessary to correct diabetes. Since those who have severe diabetes apparently age much more rapidly than normal persons, gerontologists are interested in whether such transplants will arrest aging as well as alleviate the disease. Furthermore, there is much speculation that if islet grafts work out, they may also counteract kidney damage that often forces kidney transplants on diabetics. (Scientists are even experimenting with an artificial implantable beta cell, or pancreatic cell, which contains a glucose sensor, an insulin supply and a pump. It is placed beneath the skin of the abdominal wall, is refilled by hypodermic injection, and can be recharged with a pacemaker.)

A clue to CT's mechanism may also be hidden in mysterious chemical substances called chalones. Found in cells, chalones are blocking agents that control cell proliferation. They are also tissue specific. For instance, chalones extracted from pigskin would be active in human skin; similarly, chalones in organs of animals would have mates in the corresponding human organs, and an injection of, say, animal cells complete with chalones from an animal's kidney would migrate to the human kidney — faithful to Paracelsus's dictum of *similia similibus curantur*. This explanation might support Niehans's claims that CT prevents cancer because researchers believe that when a cell loses its chalone — through trauma, carcinogen or virus — growth, including a tumor, is stimulated. Injections of chalones, which inhibit cellular growth, have brought about regression of some mouse tumors. The chalone itself does not destroy the tumor, but simply slows it down enough so that the immunological system rejects it. But the tie-in to CT may end there because Niehans's therapy is aimed at cellular revitalization, not inhibition of growth.

Quackery or cure, CT cannot be as easily dismissed as it once was. Dr. Paul Weiss, Rockefeller University's noted cell biologist, a man who watched Niehans at work, has observed that what is called cellular therapy is a wide variety of treatments by different practitioners using a number of products. Said Weiss: "Niehans admitted to me that he is no scientist, and that he doesn't know why he gives certain cells to certain people. He uses a kind of fingertip diagnosis. I would not in any way want to give the impression that I think that any of these so-called cellular therapies is valuable. I wonder that more people haven't been killed by anaphylactic shock.

But I do believe that the injection of cells into animals is worth looking into — to try to learn what happens and why. It's a field of research that should not be rejected because of the questionable behavior of the people connected with it."

Chapter Four

INFUSING HEALTHY CELLS to replace tired, old ones is not too difficult to accept for it is a form of therapy that most of us would consider logical. After all, we are conditioned for immediate effect, instant cure, and away with pain when we take medication or receive a transfusion or radiation therapy. When a physician gives us something, we expect it will help. But what if you pick up the newspaper and read an article which tells you that you might live longer if you spend a few years at the North Pole? Chances are you'd regard the suggestion as illogical.

Scientists who seek ways to lengthen the human life span are not counseling anything so simplistic as a polar vacation now and then, but they are fascinated by why cold-blooded animals such as sea tortoises live so long, and also why the same thing appears to hold true for certain warm-blooded hibernating animals. "There are no exceptions that I know of to the rule that animals live longer at lower temperatures," says Dr. Bernard L.

Strehler, professor of biology at the University of Southern California. "Among hibernating animals such as bats and hamsters, those that are forced to hibernate more often live longer, which fits in with invertebrate studies."

During natural hibernation — a period of "winter sleep" in which life is slowed and energy expenditure is reduced — body temperatures of animals such as woodchucks, ground squirrels and dormice drop to near freezing. The hibernating animals live chiefly on fats stored within their bodies, and when they emerge in the spring they are minus about thirty percent of their autumn weight. Cold, incidentally, is not always necessary to bring on such dormant states. Aestivation is a comatose state, similar to hibernation, in which many tropical animals pass the dry, hot months when food and water are unavailable. The desert mouse, for instance, goes into such a sleep, living up to four times longer than the laboratory mouse.

Such slowdowns of physiological function do not harm the animal, but they do improve longevity — so long as the animal wakes up and resumes its normal temperature every week or so. Studies have shown that hibernators cannot remain in their slowed-life condition for an indefinite period.

What the hibernator does is set a new thermostatic level for itself, a trick that makes many scientists wonder whether it might be possible to reset the thermostat in the human hypothalamus, a region at the base of the brain that regulates temperature. The hypothalamus keeps body temperature at 37° C. (98.6° F.), but lowering it a few degrees, some believe, might just be the way to extend our life spans. The idea is a viable one. But, resetting the thermostat presents several practical problems in terms of what one might do to the central nervous system and to behavior if body temperature is lowered, say, only one or two degrees. Nevertheless, temperature is one environmental factor that can be manipulated relatively easily. And in cold-blooded animals, at least, the evidence is clear. In 1917, two scientists at the Rockefeller Institute, Jacques Loeb and John H. Northrop, doubled the duration of life of fruit flies, which are cold-blooded organisms, by keeping them at 19° C. instead of their normal 25°. Loeb, a brilliant physiologist who did pioneer work on the effects of thermal, electrolytic and radiant energy on living matter, was also able, in another series of experiments, to extend the life span of sea urchin eggs a thousandfold with a similar temperature drop. More recently, UCLA's Roy Walford managed to double the life span of the tropical fish *Cynolebias* by lowering its water temperature. He observed at the same time that the fish living in the colder water grew faster and larger than those living in the warmer water. Still other experiments make use of tiny aquatic creatures called rotifers, cold-blooded animals that thrive on pond water and algae and have a normal life span of only thirty-four days — but only when the water temperature is 25° C. Increasing the water temperature about ten degrees shortens their lives to around twenty days, lowering it lengthens the span markedly, sometimes doubling it.

Some other experiments are aimed at developing an effective body-cooling drug that could be used not only to slow the aging process but to save the lives of victims of heart attack, stroke and failure of the circulatory system associated with shock. A substance that lowers metabolic rates could be injected in such cases to decrease the need for oxygen. Cell damage, thus, might be put off until emergency medical treatment became available. At Colorado State University recently, scientists turned up evidence that hibernating ground squirrels may be the source of one such temperature-lowering substance. Named antabolone, for antimetabolic hormone, it is made from the squirrels' brains. When injected into rats, it decreases their body temperatures about five degrees and slows the metabolic rate. According to Dr. Henry Swan, who has been researching the substance, at the moment it takes about ten squirrels' brains to make enough of the material to inoculate one rat. The idea, of course, is to synthesize antabolone so it may be studied more effectively. Insofar as its possible application to aging is concerned, antabolone might conceivably be used to increase the human life span by two or three times what it is now. "By taking strictly controlled doses of the substance," says Swan, "a person may be able to lower body temperature by about two degrees, which would decrease the metabolic rate by about eight percent. The result should be that the body won't wear out as fast as it does now." Swan stresses that the difficulty is that no one knows if there are harmful effects when a person is kept slightly cooled for long periods of time. In studies with mice, for example, though the animals might enjoy a lengthened life span at lower body temperatures, it has been observed that they appear drowsy and lethargic. Swan hopes that antabolone will slow the body's heat-producing mechanisms, yet not interfere with the energy producing functions that control cell survival.

Temperature manipulation can have a number of other beneficial effects. Wound healing is one, an action that may be speeded up by *raising* the temperature. Back in the 1920s, A. H. Ebeling of the Rockefeller Institute demonstrated this by making small slashes on the abdomens of young alligators, then maintaining the animals at various temperatures. At 23° C., an alligator took nearly a month to heal the gash, but when the temperature was boosted to 38° C., only eleven days were required. Induced fever also speeds up the process of phagocytosis to destroy circulating bacteria and viruses, and sometimes used in the treatment of syphilis of the nervous system. A rather interesting extension of this example of a chemical basis for cellular repair deals with the psychological appreciation of time and its chemical nature. In an effort to determine whether our perception of time is influenced by a step-up in internal secretions, the French biologist M. Marcel Francois instructed test subjects to strike a Morse key three times a second, or rather, as Lecomte du Noüy has described the experiment, the number of times which corresponded to a personal estimation of three per second. Francois then raised his subjects' body temperatures by applying electrically-generated heat. He found that when they were now asked to strike the key at the same rate as before, not only did their chemical processes speed up but they speeded up their tapping to coincide with their new idea of what was meant by one second. It is tempting to speculate what would have happened if the experiment had been carried on for years. The opposite effect of what is sometimes achieved during the slowdown of hibernation might have been the result of this alteration in inner biological and psychological time — rapid aging.

Although science has a way to go yet before it is ever able to truly extend our lives through temperature manipulation, there are already medical applications of the technique, known as inducing hypothermia. For example, temperature is often dropped during heart surgery to slow down bodily processes, making it easier to operate on the heart; ulcers are sometimes healed by treating with a hypogastric balloon filled with a supercooled fluid and swallowed by the patient. Farther out, cryonics devotees arrange to have their bodies frozen after death in the hope that science will have the expertise years hence to overcome the disease that killed them in the first place — as well as to revive them. I hasten to add that at the current state of the art, it is not an easy matter to even revive a person who has nearly frozen to death, let alone someone who has taken the big trip itself. In 1964, there was the case of a Tulsa woman found lying in a street overnight in 32-degree weather. Her body temperature dropped at least thirty-one degrees, from 98° F. to around 67° F., but one physician estimated that her temperature when she arrived at the hospital might have been as low as 59° F. Physicians made an incision in her throat to help her breathe, massaged her heart through the chest wall for two hours, forced oxygen into her lungs, electrically stimulated her heart, injected adrenaline directly into it, wrapped her in a heated blanket, and used a hypogastric balloon filled with hot water to raise the internal temperature. Seven hours later, she regained consciousness, her temperature returned to normal. Tingling fingertips and a sore throat were the only signs of her ordeal.

I said earlier that resetting our body's thermostats might affect the central nervous system and behavior. One consequence of temperature lowering in humans that is known is the effect on male virility. There is little question that the reproductive capacity of the contents of the scrotum appears to be very sensitive to even slight increases in temperature: the higher the temperature, the lower the sperm count. Dr. Howard W. Gabriel, a Kansas researcher, has told me of studies among Japanese males — who have significantly lower sperm counts than Americans — which lay the blame for their condition on the daily hot baths the Japanese typically enjoy. Other studies have examined the possibility that other factors may be responsible for the low sperm count — such things as sauna and steam baths, tight-fitting underwear, athletic supporters, electric blankets, dark-colored slacks, and localized inflammatory diseases. Dr. Gabriel has one solution: "Though the thought kind of boggles your mind perhaps, experimental studies are needed to further explore the possible therapeutic value of cold applications like ice to the scrotum. Studies might establish a new therapy for oligospermic [deficient sperm count] conditions." Voronoff and Steinach would probably have understood the potential — or rather misunderstood it — and icing the testicles might well have been a part of their rejuvenating treatment if they had known of it.

Chapter Five

AMONG THE DRUGS capable of lowering temperature, in animals, at least, is the dentist's old standby, novocaine. Indeed, all of us have heard or used the expression "The doctor will freeze it," when referring to the injection of novocaine given before a tooth is pulled or filled. Novocaine, or procaine hydrochloride as it is also known, does deaden, or "freeze," sensory nerve impulses when it is injected under the skin, into a muscle or directly into nerve trunks or beneath the membrane covering the spinal cord.

The widely-used drug, however, may do much more than deaden. It may, in fact, liven. For novocaine, it turns out, is the chief active ingredient in a controversial "youth drug" known as Gerovital H3 (GH3) which has been around for at least thirty years, for most of that time associated with the name of an energetic, seventy-ish Romanian physician, Ana Aslan. Thousands of elderly — among them Mao Tse-tung, Nikita Khrushchev and, when he wasn't undergoing cell therapy, *der Alte*, Konrad Adenauer — have traveled to Aslan's Geriatric Institute in Bucharest for injections of H3 for their senility, heart conditions, hearing difficulties, Parkinson's disease, neuralgia, baldness, arthritis, and a host of other conditions. Among the "youth therapies," it ranks second in popularity only to the Niehans treatment, despite the necessity of injections that may have to be given for life.

Researchers have known for some time that procaine could help patients suffering from arthritis and several other inflammatory diseases. Aslan, who has never really claimed discovery of the drug's positive effects in those disorders, pursued the research started and then dropped by others, confirming in her very first test that procaine did, in truth, act favorably on joint processes. A young medical student came to her clinic with arthritis of the right knee, complaining of severe pain for three weeks. Aslan shot him up with novocaine and he was immediately able to flex the knee up to ninety degrees. Aslan pressed on in an effort to determine more precisely the effect of procaine in cases of experimentally-induced arthritis, and while observing laboratory animals treated with the drug noticed some interesting "special effects." The animals put on more weight, developed shiny fur and, in those treated prophylactically with the drug, re- sistance to arthritis was greater. In eighty-five percent of all cases, complete cures were recorded. Aslan next treated elderly patients suffering from joint diseases and found that their vitality increased and their memories improved; those who had Parkinson's disease had less muscle stiffness. Encouraged by what she saw, Aslan began to investigate the effects of prolonged and periodic procaine treatment on aging itself and, at least according to her case histories, found that it had an enriching and rejuvenating effect on the patients as a whole. Their biological age actually seemed to fall below their chronological age. One dramatic example involved a ninety-one-year-old mentally disturbed woman with a litany of other problems: hearing and vision impairment, inability to care for herself and recall the names of her dead children, scaly and wrinkled skin, hypertension, arteriosclerosis, skin tumors, frequent hysterical crying, enuresis, acute arthritis, poor reflexes, heart murmur, trembling, a bent body, and completely white hair. Procaine treatment was begun in May of 1951, and by September both her skin condition and hearing had improved. By December, her muscles were stronger, her gait steadier, her body erect, and she was able to bend at the waist and touch her toes with her fingertips. She could care for herself and could now remember earlier dates and experiences. In April of the following year, the woman was taking walks into the city alone, and was capable of such delicate tasks as buttoning her clothes. By August of 1952, her reflexes were markedly improved, as was her ability to concentrate, and the color was returning to her hair. Her sclerosis had disappeared, as had the "rolling appearance" of her veins. By October, the woman's face was smooth, and by August of 1956 not only had her hair become stronger but eighty percent of its former color had returned. "Her eyelashes were completely repigmented," Aslan reported, "her gaze vivacious. The occasional episodes of depression are gone the old woman exhibits general liveliness. Several times a day she goes up and down the steps of the Institute. Her muscles show considerable development. The skin on her legs feels smooth. The woman goes out by herself, remembers new experiences and recalls episodes of the distant past."

These "antiaging" effects were not noticed by earlier researchers because, according to Aslan and her supporters, the procaine they used did not contain essential ingredients of the kind mixed into what came to be known as H3. Those ingredients probably do play an important part in making the drug effective — and there is little doubt that H3 does have several positive effects — and they are not as mysterious as some have suggested. They consist chiefly of benzoic acid, a preservative, and potassium metabisulfate, an antioxidant. Both of these keep the procaine molecule active in the system. Ordinary procaine undergoes a fairly rapid destruction at the hands of a circulating enzyme, but when it is buffered as it is in H3, it remains in the body for hours, long enough to work in the central nervous system. Furthermore, the antioxidant in the mix affects the acid-alkaline balance of the solution, making H3 more acid than procaine and thus lessening its anesthetic properties. (We'll discuss the role of antioxidants in aging in another chapter.) H3 and ordinary procaine, then, have very different pharmacological and metabolic action.

Gerovital, Aslan has explained, acts on the entire nervous system, on the hormone-producing endocrine glands and on various metabolic processes. In the body, it produces two biological agents, para-aminobenzoic acid (PABA) and diethylaminoethanol (DEAE). PABA, the ingredient in topical sunscreens that helps protect the skin against premature aging, stimulates the production of folic acid, a vitamin so essential that without it cells cannot live, and new cells cannot be manufactured to replace damaged ones. An insufficiency of folic acid in our systems can cause a number of mental changes, among them listlessness, irritability and forgetfulness. PABA also stimulates the production of vitamin K, which helps blood clot to avoid hemorrhaging, and thiamine (vitamin B), which converts sugar and starches into energy. Aslan's earlier experiments also indicated that procaine has a biocatalytic action that stimulates the growth of plants. Studying the effects of the drug on germination in beans, she and her co-workers observed that high concentrations tended to depress germination, but that low concentrations had a decidedly stimulating effect. In her other plant studies, Aslan found that soaking seeds in procaine or spraying it onto plants stimulated growth and fruit development and increased resistance to viral diseases. This biocatalytic effect, she reported, may be exerted in all tissues, including the human nervous system.

When researchers have examined genuine H3 and not simply novocaine — and several serious studies are currently under way in the United States under FDA approval — they have turned up enough positive results to at least partly confirm Aslan's contentions. Even a generally negative Soviet study recently grudgingly conceded that H3 had a mild antidepressant effect, if not a beneficial physiological one. Quite possibly, the Russian scientists were not interested in finding any worth in the drug, particularly since Khrushchev took it and the image of a vigorous former premier was hardly palatable to those who helped force him into seclusion.

In 1973, at the Gerontological Society meeting, a group of American investigators reported on their studies with Gerovital, and while there was no ringing endorsement of the drug, some indicated that it may do something on the cellular level to modify some of the problems of aging. One of the more optimistic presentations was by Dr. Keith S. Ditman, medical director of the Vista Hill Psychiatric Foundation in San Diego, and Dr. Sidney Cohen, adjunct professor of psychiatry at UCLA. They gave intramuscular injections of H3 to forty-one subjects ranging in age from forty to eighty-five, people who were either normal volunteers or who had psychiatric or medical problems. Of the forty-one, thirty-five reported improvement. Most said they slept better, were less depressed, and had a heightened sense of well-being. There was also a noticeable decline in the serum cholesterol levels of eight of nine patients who had tested high in that category before the H3 experiment, as well as relief from arthritis and neuritis. "Such broad claims of improvement are intriguing and encouraging," Ditman reported, "but caution in their interpretation is indicated. The possibility of a psychogenic effect cannot be ruled out, particularly when a well-heralded drug such as Gerovital is administered. The need for double-blind controlled studies is apparent." (Nearly all of the subjects in the study were aware of the drug's reputation and had volunteered for that reason.)

Another report dealt with aged red blood cells which become rigid in the laboratory if kept at body temperature for twenty-four hours. Dr. R. F. Baker of the University of Southern California School of Medicine said he was able to alter that rigidity by treating the cells with H3. Also on the cellular level, Dr. J. E. Officer of USC's pathology department treated mouse cell cultures with H3 and found that while it slowed the growth of young cells, the rate of division was renewed in older cells comparable to the rate of the younger.

Dr. B. M. Zuckerman of the University of Massachusetts investigated the effect of H3 on aging and reproduction of nematodes, microscopic worms. As these worms age, they become more dense and fragile, and will burst when placed in certain solutions. Although H3 did not seem to affect the worms' longevity, it did significantly retard the arrival of both density and fragility. They stayed supple longer than untreated worms. Gerovital also got good marks as an antidepressant in 1974 after a double-blind study — one in which neither doctor nor patient knows what drug the patient is taking until the study is over — at Duke University Medical Center. Dr. William K. Zung, a professor of psychiatry, and six other Duke doctors, gave H3 to patients sixty-one to seventy-seven years of age. All had symptoms of depression, including confusion, hopelessness, unexplained fatigue and tearfulness. Other depressed patients from sixty to seventy-nine got placebos, or took imipramine, a drug known to create feelings of well-being. Halfway through the two-month trial, H3 patients had become noticeably more cheerful and optimistic — as did those on imipramine but less dramatically so.

No one is quite certain how H3 works as an antidepressant, but there is speculation that it is possibly a so-called MAO inhibitor. MAO, or monoamine oxidase, is an enzyme that begins piling up in the brain in middle age. It interferes with vital substances such as noradrenaline, a hormone whose actions are similar to that of adrenaline. Noticeably high levels of MAO have turned up in the brains of depressed and even schizophrenic individuals, and the suggestion is that the enzyme displaces brain chemicals essential to mental balance and well-being. By suppressing, or inhibiting, the MAO enzyme with various drugs it is possible to treat depression and some forms of psychosis. H3 seems to do just that.

One of H3's advantages over other antidepressants is the virtual absence of side effects with its use. Others may produce hypertension, abnormally low blood pressure or dizziness. "Basically, MAO breaks down one compound, let's call it compound A," explains Duke's Zung. "Compound A is what you need lots of and a lack of it produces emotional depression. One way of treating depression is to inhibit this breakdown, and that's what Gerovital may be doing."

Whether Gerovital is a true rejuvenator as well as an antidepressant is another matter. Aslan (who, incidentally, has been taking it herself for years) and her supporters contend that it is, arguing not only that depres-

sion and aging are bedfellows but that when we age
there is always a rise in MAO activity and a closely-linked
decline in noradrenaline. Not everyone agrees. At the
1973 gerontology meeting on H3, Dr. Alvin I. Goldfarb
of Mount Sinai Hospital in New York, one of the more
vocal critics of the drug, declared: "The drug was ini-
tially promoted for use in this country and elsewhere as
a rejuvenant. Later, the claim was switched from rejuvenant to a retardant of aging. When we contested
this, the claim was changed to, 'It's a prophylactic.' How
are you going to test prophylaxis against aging? We'd
need millions of subjects." Goldfarb added that if Gerovital gets FDA approval as an antidepressant, it will
come on the market and old people will press for it.
"But younger people will be taking it too," he added.
"Because they'll say, 'What can we lose, it's harmless.'"
Another critic is Zhores A. Medvedev, the eminent Russian-born biologist, now exiled and working at the
National Institute for Medical Research in London. Medvedev, who is also skeptical of reports of supercentenarians living in the Caucasus, says that the publicity given
in the Soviet press to Romanian efforts to prolong the life
span induced the Soviet Ministry of Health to establish
the Research Institute of Gerontology in Kiev whose first
project was the introduction of procaine therapy. But
after several years, says Medvedev, the research was
dropped because of negative conclusions. "An explanation for the difference in efficiency of the method in
Romania and the Soviet Union was discovered," the
biologist claims, "but never published, since it was rather
delicate from the political point of view. In Romania, the

Aslan clinic procured most of its patients from old-age institutions where conditions and medical care for the aged and often homeless people left much to be desired. Once placed in a first-rate government clinic, these patients responded very positively to procaine injections combined with vitamins and good care. In the Soviet Union, the first people to undergo revitalization therapy were top-ranking government and party officials, including Nikita Khrushchev himself. Procaine injections produced no objective 'revitalization' effects in them, only temporary euphoria."

Nonetheless, while H3's effectiveness as general therapy for aging is still unclear, its antidepressant capability is not. It is also heartening to note, too, that the U.S. medical profession seems to have dropped its almost paranoid attitude toward Aslan and H3. In 1956, when she first reported in a German medical journal that she had brought about phenomenal improvement in the mental, physiological, and social functioning of 189 elderly patients who had undergone H3 therapy for ten years, the muttering she set off in the scientific community was hardly evidence of an idea whose time had come. Three years later, after her address before the International Association of Gerontology in San Francisco, she was branded an outright fraud. "If these claims were true," one prominent gerontologist declared, "you'd be adding ten years to your life every time a dentist filled a tooth. This woman is the Pied Piper of the Sixties, leading the aged instead of the young." Today, that same scientist concedes privately that his remark was intemperate and that H3 may have some value after all. Recently, too, a reputable American medical news magazine, discussing the favorable results of U.S. studies of H3, saw fit to report on the case of a seventy-nine-year-old American physician who took the drug himself from a large supply he brought back from Romania years before and who "fishes, hunts, skis and makes love twice a week and feels wonderful."

Part III

Slowing the Clock

Introduction

MOST OF THE ATTEMPTS at rejuvenation that we have discussed thus far fall into the category of symptom relievers. As promising as H3 might be, as logical as CT seems to some, neither has favorably altered the life expectancy charts to any noticeable degree. They will probably never do that. All we can say about current efforts to actually do something about aging is that they are purely speculative, or simply still experimental. They are, when there have been some indications of success, merely ways of keeping us from growing tired too quickly.

All of the changes that come with aging can be modified to some extent. We can take medications, have operations, avoid smog and radiation, and watch our diets. If we do enough of these things in time, we will probably make it through life as sound of mind and body as it is humanly possible to do so. But what these measured steps will not do is give us immortality — it is difficult to conceive of anything beyond spiritual intervention that will do that — or anything more than a few extra years of healthier existence. For all of the nasty changes that appear as we grow old — the senile cataracts and dementia, the dried skin, stiffened joints and dimmed eye and gastrointestinal complaints — are superimposed on what we have referred to as the biological clock. The signs of aging are, indeed, like the scratched paint and the tarnished finish and the sluggish works of a worn clock. Beneath those defects, the timepiece continues to tick away the hours that have been wound into it. No wood polish, no face soap can make it run efficiently. Only a watch repairman skilled enough in the inner workings of this delicate instrument that measures out our hours can do that. If ever science is to find a way to stop us from aging, it must first learn how the biological clock runs, then it must find out how to slow it down. For the clock does exist, in every living thing, setting a time for flowers to open and close, oysters to sleep and awaken, infants to cry for a feeding. Without knowledge of the clock, without tinkering with its works, any effort to deal with the aging process itself is pointless. For aging is the result of fundamental biological events that require a deep understanding of such things as hormone balances, changes in the body's immune system, collagen chemistry, oxidative reactions, and lastly, the structure and regulation of our genes and the various other constituents of the cell. Some of these are poorly understood, even today; others have had much of the fog burned from around them.

So basic an approach to aging is necessarily a slow process as each scientist adds to the knowledge pool, step by step. Few, if any, researchers in aging would care to deviate from their commitment to supply bits and pieces of accurate information, because they are, for the most part, basic scientists, men and women not so much interested in the direct application of their work to human needs as they are in explaining the whys and hows of nature. This is not to say that they do not care about being of use to humankind. I doubt that there is any piece of research, no matter how abstruse, that does not have some significance or application to humanity. It is more a matter of priority. The basic scientist is not, contrary to popular opinion, learning more and more about less and less. It is just that he or she is only secondarily interested in harnessing the data. Basic scientists working in gerontology are aware that landing men on the moon, producing polio and other vaccines, and building heart-lung and kidney dialysis machines are triumphs of applied research. But they are also aware — and their work is paced by the understanding — that in each instance a knowledge base had to be constructed first.

Research on the aging front has become an area of growing importance. This is evident in the recent creation of the National Institute on Aging within the National Institutes of Health, and the establishment of several college programs in gerontology where there were virtually none a few years ago. The biomedical research currently under way is divided into two broad categories — the mechanisms of aging and the interaction of aging with external influences. The first of these, as set forth in the NIA's 1977 research plan, covers a broad range from molecular genetics to the clinical aspects of disease in the elderly; the second analyzes the influences on aging of diet and nutrition, drugs and their metabolism, and a variety of other chemical and physical factors. The approaches in both categories stretch from the very fundamental to the applied, and they include the biology of aging cells, longitudinal studies of aging populations, basic immunology, analyzing the response of the elderly to primary and secondary infections, analysis of cell structures, and studies of the effects of different diets on resistance to diseases.

Many organisms besides humans are used in aging research, and some of these play key roles, as we shall see in the pages ahead. These include primates, pedigreed dogs, rats and mice, metazoa such as nematodes, protozoa such as the ciliates and the amoebas, and cultured mammalian cells. Rats and mice are widely used in aging research because they have short lives, cost comparatively little, and can be genetically defined. Moreover, colonies of rodents and subhuman primates can be reproducibly maintained in institutional and commercial facilities for shipment to investigators.

The need for such research should, of course, be obvious. A healthier, stronger, and longer-living population is a most desirable end, and only laboratory research can provide it. But, ultimately, research will not do the job alone, for if the quality of human life is to be enhanced along with its quantity, other supports will be essential. This theme will be expanded upon later. Suffice it to say now that unless enlightened public policymakers, social agencies, and economic institutions back the fruits of research teams, all the tinkering with nematodes, mice, and monkeys will never move beyond the laboratory or from the pages of the journals which scientists use to talk to themselves.

Chapter Six

WHEN BROWN-SEQUARD was injecting testicular extract into himself he was, unwittingly, paving the way for what we now know as organotherapy, the treatment of human diseases with extracts of animal tissue such as thyroid and ovarian hormones.

Hormones are chemical "messengers" that the glands secrete into the bloodstream to help regulate the function of our cells and organs and control growth and energy. Traveling rapidly in the blood's flow, each carries a special message to various sites in the body — changing what we eat into muscle and blood, bone and brain, making us short or tall, regulating our heartbeats, affecting our personalities, determining our sexual behavior and controlling our fertility. Besides the ones we know of, there are others speeding about in our bodies, waiting to be discovered, probably controlling functions whose mechanisms of action still remain a mystery.

Hormones, of course, are used to treat the conditions

and changes commonly seen in the aged. Since the production of sex hormones does drop off with advancing age in men and women, hormone replacement can help in treating male climacteric and female menopause, but this does not mean that aging is a product of sexual dysfunction. Often, declining sexual powers (or the feeling that they are declining) is brought on by physical or psychological difficulties not related to endocrine malfunction.

Hormone therapy is not a rejuvenator of the Brown-Séquard variety, although testosterone injections may be administered to elderly males to treat progressive impotence (which occasionally responds to such therapy) or to remedy a hormone deficiency and improve the general state of health. But therapy of this sort must be handled carefully since male hormones may depress the production of sperm or, more seriously, induce prostatic cancer. Female hormones are often prescribed for women to help them cope with the metabolic changes and the emotional crises that may occur when ovarian activity ceases with menopause. Also, since menopause appears to increase a woman's chances of developing atherosclerosis because ovarian hormones may regulate the level of cholesterol in the blood, some physicians administer female estrogens — no longer produced in menopausal women or in women whose ovaries have been removed — to prevent or inhibit the hardening of arteries caused by cholesterol deposits. In this sense, administration of a hormone might be considered a way to prolong life by delaying or halting the onset of a prime killer. (Giving female hormones to males for the same reason is not such a good idea because they produce severe feminizing side effects.)

While hormones have much to do with some of the symptoms of aging, a direct relationship between the potent chemicals and the actual aging process has not yet been demonstrated. A number of scientists feel, however, that such a tie-in is possible. Before examining that relationship, some background material on the brain — which gerontologists see as the place from which aging changes might be directed — may be useful. A three-pound electrochemical instrument, the adult human brain has ten billion neurons, or nerve cells, that lie close together in the gray matter of the cortex, sending signals pulsing across the 400-billionths-of-an-inch gaps, or synapses, that separate them. Synonymous with the mind, with intelligence, memory, judgment, learning and creativity, the brain is a complex of numerous specialized regions, the product of two billion years of evolutionary isolation in the bony encasement of the skull. Every time we hate, love, fear, and crave, it is elaborately at work, controlling our dreams, our fantasies, our real behavior. Connected to all parts of the body by nerves, this rather unattractive spongy web of cells is tuned in whenever we move, feel, hear, speak, see, write, and breathe. It beams its electrochemical messages between head and toe, and these bursts of activity when neurons fire go on every moment of our lives, waking or sleeping. Step on a tack, goes the classic grade school example, and pain nerves are activated. The neurons are stimulated, and they send an electrical message to the brain, warning it of unpleasantness. Instantly, the brain sends a message back to the foot muscles, ordering them to pull the foot away. These messages are carried by brain chemicals called neurotransmitters. Among these are noradrenaline, serotonin, and biogenic amines, which are released into the infinitesimal synapses to either stimulate or inhibit the adjacent neuron's physiological activity. The system over which all of this works is a delicate and complicated network with branches in every part of the body. Actually, the network is a meshing of two systems — the nervous system and the hormone-releasing endocrine system — and each is capable of exerting an effect on the other.

First, the nervous system. There are two main divisions, central and autonomic. The latter is subdivided into two other systems, sympathetic and parasympathetic, which meticulously balance each other to keep the body on a healthy, steady course. The central nervous system, made up of the brain and spinal cord, supervises all of our voluntary activities — our muscular movements, consciousness and mental activity. The autonomic system, linked by nerves to the central system, takes care of our involuntary actions — those things our bodies must do, such as heart and lung action, the digestive process, operation of the glands, and function of the smooth muscle tissue of hollow organs. This control by the autonomic nervous system is exerted over nerves that feed from both the parasympathetic and sympathetic divisions directly into the body's internal organs, among them the heart, intestines, stomach, liver, pancreas, bladder, reproductive organs, kidneys, and salivary glands.

The sympathetic division of the autonomic system

may be likened to the accelerator of an automobile, particularly in an emergency situation. In times of stress, for instance, it reacts by, in effect, stepping on the gas, thus flooding the bloodstream with adrenaline (epinephrine), a hormone manufactured by the endocrine glands that constricts the blood vessels and drives up blood pressure. The heart beats faster, the pupils of the eyes dilate, the muscles tense. Gastric juices and the involuntary muscle movement in our intestines that propels food along are inhibited. Digestion is impaired.

Enter the parasympathetic system. It works hard to restore the balance that has been upset by the sympathetic's somewhat heavy-handed response. And it ultimately wins out. Under its direction, the heartbeat is slowed, blood pressure drops, the pupils constrict, and the secretions of most glands are stimulated.

Tied into all of this, as we noted earlier, is the endocrine system of glands. This includes the thyroid, parathyroids, pineal, adrenals, thymus, ovaries, testes and pituitary. It is the pituitary, the linchpin of the endocrine system, and its governor, the hypothalamus, on which gerontologists interested in the various brain-hormone theories of aging concentrate. The hypothalamus is the body's heat-regulating center. Situated in front of the brain stem just above the pituitary, it is jam-packed with nerve centers that monitor blood pressure and body temperature, regulate sexual activity, hunger, thirst, the wake-sleep cycle, water balance, sweat glands, and digestion. When electrically stimulated, furthermore, it triggers a broad range of sensations and emotional reactions in both animals and humans — intense pleasure, terror, rage, anxiety, and calm. It does this with its own special chemicals that activate or prevent the release of various hormones from the pea-sized pituitary to which it is connected by nerve fibers. These hormones, in turn, travel through the bloodstream until they reach the other endocrine glands, which are stimulated to release their own hormones. These new hormones then go on to perform an incredible array of chores that regulate the activities of cells and organs and control various physiological and emotional functions.

The endocrine glands are really tissue capsules crisscrossed with blood vessels. As we have indicated, the hormones they secrete into the bloodstream have much to do with growth and sexual development, reproduction, metabolism, liver and kidney function, heartbeat, digestion, the timing of puberty and menopause, skin coloring, how sluggish or energetic we are. They muster our defenses, emotional and immunological, they affect our personalities and behavior. To name but a few: vasopressin, secreted by the pituitary, causes the kidneys to reabsorb water, preventing the excess excretion of urine that is known as diuresis, and also constricts the blood vessels, driving up blood pressure; cortisone, from the adrenal glands, influences the rate our bodies use sugar, proteins and fats, and it governs mineral balance; thyroxine, from the thyroid gland, controls the production of heat and energy in the tissues. When we are well, it is a sign that the entire delicate system is in perfect balance; when we are not, *it* is not, for each gland affects the other.

The network is a little like a sequential set of Christmas tree lights. The wall socket is the hypothalamus, supplying the power; the plug at the end of the string of lights is the pituitary. When all functions as it should, every bulb remains lighted; a problem with the socket, the plug or just one bulb knocks the system out or causes it to flicker. Underactivity or overactivity of one gland affects the quantity of hormone it sends out to another, in turn affecting *its* output; excessive production or deficiency then results in disease. Excessive parathyroid hormone, for instance, sends increased levels of calcium from the bones to the blood and urine, resulting in the formation of kidney stones and softening of the bones (osteoporosis), a condition most often seen in people of very advanced age. Underactivity of the adrenals produces Addison's disease, a rare disorder marked by low blood pressure, weakness, anemia, and irritability; an overactive thyroid makes one hyperactive and nervous; underactivity of the thyroid causes fatigue and weight gain.

Chemistry, then, is at the core of all of the foregoing. Brain chemistry, to be specific. The aforementioned biogenic amines, for example, have been connected to mood and emotional states. Scientists now believe that certain drugs that can elevate or depress mood seem to have some effect on key brain chemicals such as the amines. Just how this occurs is not clear, but it is known that the mood-elevating drugs tend to speed up the activity of some amines, while the mood-depressing drugs slow them down. At Princeton, scientists produced some interesting reactions with a drug, carbachol, which imitates the action of a suspected neurotransmitter. Twelve rats that never kill mice were injected with the drug in the brain area responsible for emotion. Every rat proceeded to kill mice placed in its cage. Further, the drug-induced killing had the same appearance as a natural killing, that is, the kill was made with a bite through the cervical spinal cord even though the animals had neither killed before nor had seen other rats kill. When scientists reversed the process, by injecting killer rats with a substance that blocked the action of the brain chemical mimicked by carbachol, mice placed in the cages of the killers were sniffed and stalked, but not attacked.

Brain chemistry may also be changed every time we eat a meal, and these changes, it has been suggested by scientists at the Massachusetts Institute of Technology, may affect such behaviors as appetite, sexual activity, sleep, and glandular secretions. Drs. John D. Fernstrom and Richard J. Wurtman reported recently that dietary carbohydrates cause the amount of the neurotransmitter serotonin to increase rapidly. Consumption of dietary proteins, on the other hand, has the opposite effect. Because of this, the researchers theorized that changes in brain serotonin caused by eating certain foods allow neurons containing this compound to "sense" the state of bodily metabolism, and to help the brain decide whether to be hungry or to sleep, and so on. The MIT chemists' findings are remarkable because brain scientists always thought that organ was unaffected by short-term blood chemistry fluctuations caused by eating or by brief periods of fasting. They used to believe that the only time the brain was really vulnerable to such influences was in the case of prolonged malnutrition.

Brain chemists now know that the amount of a neurotransmitter in the brain affects the activity of our nerve cells, and that when a particular treatment increases or decreases the level of the chemical, it causes a corresponding change in the amount of neurotransmitter released. Injecting insulin, for example, elevates the levels of both brain serotonin and tryptophan, an essential amino acid normally found in the blood. The same thing occurs when insulin is normally secreted after one eats a carbohydrate meal. This action is proof that a hormone can control the amount of neurotransmitter in the brain.

The connection between aging and hormones, as we have said, centers on the hypothalamus and the pituitary, the two key elements in the endocrine-nervous system complex. The relationship is not one of direct cause and effect; that is, no one can say that too much or too little of one hormone or another is what makes us age. On the other hand, there are some interesting indirect tie-ins that are worth mentioning. Consider, for instance, the Pacific salmon, which degenerates rapidly as it struggles inland to spawn. Researchers have recently found that its pituitary works erratically, speeding up metabolism and eating up body fat. In a few short weeks, this fish loses its beautiful, shiny, orange-red color and changes into a dull, deteriorated creature with all of the outward signs of age. After spawning, it dies. Some other interesting correlations between endocrine secretions and aging have turned up in studies of growth hormone from the pituitary. At the University of California in the 1940s, Dr. Herbert M. Evans (who discovered the hormone in 1921) began with two groups of full-grown rats ranging in age from 192 to 221 days — a human equivalent of about twenty-five to thirty years. The average weight of one group was about eight ounces, the other, nine. Each day, the nine-ounce rats got an injection of hormone. By the time the rats were an average of 647 days old (about seventy-five to eighty years in humans), the injected ones had reached the stature of giants, with an average weight of over a pound and three ounces, or, more than twice that of normal full-grown weight. The animals' flesh remained lean and the bones did not undergo the changes ordinarily seen in aging. Evans discovered also that the injected rats excreted less nitrogen in body wastes than did the normal rats. Since nitrogen is a necessary constituent of amino acids, its lower level in the excretions indicated that the growth hormone allowed the rats to use the normally wasted amount of the element to build extra protein. In another experiment, Evans removed the pituitary glands from a pair of young dachshunds and injected one of the animals with an extract made from canine pituitaries. Its muscles, bones and fatty tissues grew steadily until at maturity it was double the size of its litter mate who had received no injections. Nowadays, human growth hormone, HGH, is used to treat children severely stunted by hypopituitarism. One of ten hormones produced by the pituitary, HGH increases the level of sugar in the blood for energy, and helps accumulate the protein-building amino acids. If these results are applicable to aging humans, we might someday be able to take growth hormone as we now take vitamins to retard the wasting process that is part of aging.

Another hormone link to growth and aging, and one that has provided many gerontologists searching for a youth-promoting substance with a fairly bright laboratory beacon, was turned up by Dr. V. B. Wigglesworth, a British zoologist and authority on metamorphosis. This is the process by which many insects, amphibians and mollusks progress, in distinct stages, from egg to adult. Evans severed the head of a species of insect during its larval stage, discovering that this caused the body to change quickly into an adult. Reasoning that the head contained some sort of inhibitor, he dissected it and found a pair of tiny glands which secrete a substance known as juvenile hormone. As long as the glands produce the substance, metamorphosis is postponed, but when they quit — as they normally do after a time — the insect undergoes the striking changes that bring it to the mature, reproductive adult stage. Transplanting the glands of a young larva into an old one also slows down metamorphosis, a finding that has spurred several investigators to hunt for a substance that imitates juvenile hormone's ability to extend the youthful stage. But there is another noteworthy sidelight to the juvenile hormone story. At Harvard a few years ago, two biologists working with a European insect, *Pyrrhocoris apterus,* noticed that it was not transforming into a sexually mature adult at the end of its fifth larval stage. In fact, all 1,500 of the insects reared at the laboratory continued to grow as larvae instead of metamorphosing into adults, forming giant but immature larvae which finally died without being able to produce. This is exactly what would have happened if the bugs had been treated with their own juvenile hormone. The researchers, Dr. Karel Slama and Professor Carroll M. Williams, began to search for the source of the hormone — finally tracking it to a small piece of ordinary paper toweling that had been placed in each rearing jar. When the paper was removed, the juvenile hormone effect disappeared, and all the insects developed normally. Next, the biologists tested twenty other brands of American towels and tissues by simply letting the immature bugs walk on them. Eighteen of the twenty brands showed high juvenile hormone activity, proving that it was widespread in American paper products. "Indeed," Slama and Williams reported, "pieces of American newspapers and journals, among them the *New York Times, Wall Street Journal, Science and Scientific American,* showed extremely high juvenile hormone activity. The London *Times* and *Nature* were inactive, and so were other paper materials of European or Japanese manufacture." Partially purified extract of the hormone proved to be incredibly active when applied to any part of the unbroken skin of the European insect. And, the scientists calculated, one ounce would block the metamorphosis and cause the death of three billion of them. The implications for insect control are, of course, enormous. And though their work had nothing to do with gerontology, one can speculate, nevertheless, how substances that act like juvenile hormone to preclude development — if they could be synthesized and their action carefully controlled — may be used to arrest aging in humans. The irony is that newspapers and scientific journals, which aim to stimulate intellectual growth through the dissemination of information, should be the source of an inhibiting factor. Indeed, contrary to the publications' detractors, they might well be worth the paper they are printed on.

Because thyroid hormone is the main regulator of cellular metabolic rate, and because aging is associated with a slowing of cellular metabolism, several researchers are looking at how age might affect the way the gland produces or releases thyroxine hormone. Some of the studies have already shown that the thyroid in older people is capable of releasing an adequate amount of hormone, but the rate which the elderly can utilize it is lower than in the young. Some aging symptoms, then, might be caused not by the inability of the body to synthesize hormones but, rather, by its growing lack of efficiency in using them. Other studies indicate that thyroid glands in the elderly can, in fact, be made to release increased amounts of hormone by prodding them with a shot of thyroid-stimulating hormone (TSH).

Another clue to the association between aging and hormones may be found in the female's favored position over the male with respect to longevity. Scientists would like to know why females of many species live longer than males, and there is a suspicion that the sex hormones play a significant part. Some years ago, for example, Cornell researchers administered female hormones to male and female rats and found that their lives could be prolonged in this fashion. Male hormones, however, cut their life spans. In a similar, more drastic line of research, other investigators castrated kokanee salmon before the start of their gonadal development and discovered that the operation prolonged their life spans. It has also been demonstrated that castrated cats live longer than normal male cats, with an even greater extension of life if castration occurs before maturation rather than afterwards. What is true for cats and salmon even appears to be true for man, and the hormones that make him masculine may also be trimming years from his life. Dr. James B. Hamilton of State University of New York Downstate Medical Center looked into this matter of female longevity and noted that most of the major causes of death in humans occur more commonly or at an earlier age in males than in females. Moreover, males are "penalized" by the great majority of those diseases which occur more frequently in one sex. The difference, Hamilton theorized, is likely to become even greater in the future since males are less able than females to take advantage of improvements that promote longevity.

One explanation of man's greater vulnerability blames it on the lack of a second X chromosome — which is the normal female complement. Men have only one X and a much smaller Y, a situation that may shorten life because the smaller Y chromosome lacks some genes. There are some creatures, however, in which the male outlives the female. Among these are mallard ducks and songbirds. Another theory implicates sex hormones, particularly the androgens produced by the testes.

The fact that castration apparently increases life span gives further support to the second theory, according to Hamilton. He conducted a long-term study of inmates in an institution for the mentally retarded. More than 700 of his subjects were intact males, 297 were eunuchs.

Each eunuch was matched closely with the other males for such things as year of birth and length of hospitalization. The upshot was strikingly longer life among the castrates than among the normals — 69.3 years for eunuchs, 55.7 for the intact men. Hamilton's studies also showed that there was a lower percentage of deaths in castrated males than in intact females, and that castration was associated with fewer deaths from infections along with an older mean age at death from infection. "The fact that the percentage of dead subjects was lower in eunuchs than in women," Hamilton summed up, "does not necessarily indicate that female sex hormones produced by the ovaries shorten life. Consideration may be given to the androgens known to be secreted by human ovaries."

The data from these castration studies would appear to contradict Voronoff's belief that men "fortunately endowed" with active genitals were assured of extended youth and longer life spans. Voronoff wrongly zeroed in on the physical signs of aging his eunuchs displayed and forgot, it seems, to take their life spans into account. Nevertheless, it is doubtful that any physician today would seriously consider castration as a cure for a short life.

The role of the hypothalamus in aging, it should be obvious from all of the foregoing, is an important one. Some gerontologists believe, in fact, that it may be the prime mover in the process, actually pacing the rate at which aging changes occur through the signals it sends to the endocrine glands. One example of this involves the ovaries, which quit producing estrogen after menopause and become scar tissue. As a result of the cessation, the uterus, fallopian tubes, and vagina become atrophied, and a number of other changes, physical and emotional, take place; the skin loses its suppleness, the hair its sheen, the bones their calcium and protein. There may be deepening depression, increased irritability, hot flashes and dizziness. It is all much like what Voronoff observed in his eunuchs. These events, in a sense premature aging, are hardly the same as those that occur during puberty even though the same control center, the hypothalamus, is busy working. What seems to happen is that increased amounts of some agent within the central nervous system goads the hypothalamus into altering the signals it sends to the ovaries and other endocrine glands during pubescence, thus causing many, if not all, of the changes of aging. The best bet about the identity of the prodding agent is our old friend, MAO, monoamine oxidase, which breaks down the message-laden neurotransmitters, the biogenic amines. (You'll recall, in our discussion of Gerovital, that MAO begins piling up in our brains in middle age, interfering with hormones and other vital substances.)

The hypothalamus may also be stimulated to act in certain ways by applying electrical current to it, a response that buttresses the argument of scientists who believe in a central pacemaker of aging located in the brain area. For instance, in experiments with aged rats, researchers have succeeded in restoring function to the animals' ovaries by applying minute currents of electricity to their hypothalami. They have done the same thing with injections of hormones and brain chemicals. Other scientists have removed the pituitary glands from young female rats, replaced them with pituitaries from older rats — and watched the young animals' ovaries age prematurely. They have injected L-Dopa, the drug used to treat Parkinson's disease patients, into aging female rats and increased their fertility, thus suggesting that something wrong with the hypothalamus — not with the sex organs — is behind reproductive problems. And when they transplant tired ovaries from old rats into young ones, they produce fertile eggs. All of these events are proof, say some gerontologists, that a central pacemaker in the hypothalamus — not the reproductive system by itself — is running at least part of the aging process, if only the part that deals with the reproductive system. Extrapolating from that, scientists speculate that the hypothalamus, with its acknowledged awesome power, is somehow able to control all of the other body systems that run down with age and eventually quit altogether. This theory is not so wild when one considers that the hypothalamus is so intimately involved, through its governing position in the hormone-nervous system, with such vital activities as heartbeat, infection control, the onset of puberty and menopause and with our general physical and mental well-being.

Chapter Seven

AS WE GROW OLDER, we become more susceptible to disease. No question about it. As we lose irreplaceable brain cells, and the balance of our chemical neurotransmitters shifts, as a host of other invisible changes takes place in cells everywhere in our bodies, we cannot help being affected in adverse ways, mentally and physically. Whether all of the problems that come as we "age out" do so *because* of the advancing years, or merely *with* them, is a difficult question to answer. Distinguishing aging from the diseases of aging is, as we have said, no easy task. Many diseases, of course, do not strike us simply because we are old. Atherosclerosis, or hardening of the arteries, is one of these. It is found in the very young, and so, too, are arthritis and diabetes. Unfortunately, physicians and the elderly themselves too often blame "aging" for a wide variety of symptoms, throw up their hands in frustration and fail to treat illness that is treatable.

Nevertheless, we cannot forget that aging *does* result from many biological changes within us all, and the fact of aging, therefore, can and does bear upon the symptoms, the course of disease in the elderly, and on how effective treatment will be. Without knowing just what changes do occur with age, scientists would be hard-pressed to find their causes, nor would they be able to determine what is normal and what is abnormal in an old person. Studying the diseases of aging themselves is an essential way of understanding the aging process since the two are so often intertwined. Or, as someone has put it: "Nature nowhere so reveals her usual workings as when she deviates from her usual paths." What the researchers into aging must do is examine those diseases of aging, and try to tie them to the genetic changes that occur on the microscopic biological level over time. If they can do this, what is ultimately gained is a better understanding of how heredity and environment team up to influence the various age-associated ills that plague and will plague us all.

It is to the body's immunological system, the system that guards us against disease, that researchers are turning with growing interest for clues to the causes of a number of diseases and to the process of aging itself. For the efficiency of that system declines with age, in animals and in humans, and associated with that decline — maybe causally related to it — is an increase in immunologically-related diseases.

The defense system itself works like this. It has a front line made up of protein molecules called antibodies. Produced by white blood cells, these defenders destroy or immobilize invading pathogens such as bacteria and viruses — microorganisms that carry the protein substances known as antigens. The so-called antibody-antigen reaction is best observed when tissues are set upon by bacteria through a wound in the skin. The body immediately activates its defenders and sends them to the wound where they recognize the invaders as "not self" and press the attack. Allergies, too, involve the immune system. Allergens such as pollen, house dust and some foods — substances harmless to the nonallergic — sensitize susceptible individuals. The subsequent antibody-antigen reaction releases the chemical histamine causing swelling and other irritation. Once stimulated by the antigens, the antibodies presumably "memorize" the makeup of the particular invaders, storing the profile in the cells. Then the next time the same antigens enter the body, a booster response is triggered within a half hour, and antibody production commences. Put another way, specific antigens stimulate the production of specific antibody response to them and them only. This explains the selective characteristic of immunity and why, for example, a person may be immune to measles and not to chicken pox. Attenuated vaccines, which contain a reduced potency disease organism or its toxin, build up bodily resistance against the bacteria by building up antibodies. Repeated injections often confer immunity to specific diseases.

Beneficial when arrayed against invading toxins, this defense line may prove a hindrance when kidneys, hearts and other organs are transplanted. The recipient's immune system soon recognizes the graft as "not self" and sends its disease fighters into the breach to force rejection of the foreign tissue. To halt this process, potent immunosuppressive drugs are administered to the graft recipient, a procedure that weakens the body's defenses to such an extent that, unfortunately, infective agents as well as the transplanted organ are undisturbed. Interestingly, the rejection phenomenon does not work in the case of pregnancy, when the fetus, with half of its genes foreign to the mother, remains comfortably in the womb for up to nine months.

Scientists have implicated the immune system in such common disorders as arthritis, multiple sclerosis, and cancer, and to other less well known afflictions, including common variable hypogammaglobulinemia (CVH) and systemic lupus erythematosus (SLE). Take, for instance, the case of CVH, a rare immune-deficiency disease that sometimes leads to cancer and is marked by an inability to manufacture antibodies. For a number of years, Dr. Thomas A. Waldmann and his colleagues at the National Cancer Institute studied patients, mostly children, afflicted with CVH at the NIH Clinical Center. Fifty patients had been treated, and all suffered recurrent severe infections, particularly pneumonia. Most of the victims also developed other lung diseases, thirty percent developed arthritis and ten percent, cancer. After a series of experiments, the investigators discovered that the patients' immune defect, and hence their susceptibility to disease, was caused by an excess of a type of white blood cell known as the T-cell. These cells are made in the thymus gland, a tiny bit of tissue nestled beneath the breastbone and long believed to play a minor bodily role but now known to be a mainspring in the immune system. The investigators found that the T-cells, also known as killer cells because of their genetic mandate to seek out and wreak havoc with transplanted organs and cancer cells, blocked production of defender antibodies by one of its allies against disease, the B-cell. These are produced in the bone marrow just prior to adolescence. Normally, when an antigen invades an organism, T- and B-cells form a united front against it. But in test after test, B-cells produced fewer disease-fighting antibodies when they were mixed into cultures from CVH patients that had excessive T-cells. The NIH scientists postulate that normal persons are capable of producing adequate amounts of T-cells in response to disease-bearing agents, but that abnormal T-cell production in such diseases as CVH prevents their B-cells from maturing into fully competent antibody-producing cells. This weakens children who have the disease and makes them vulnerable to infections and other ailments.

The findings may also have some relevance to other disorders associated with abnormal antibody production. One of these is SLE, a chronic inflammatory disease of the arthritis family that affects the connective tissue and blood vessels. With its classic butterfly-shaped facial rash, it strikes mostly young women, may become worse from exposure to the sun, and is liable to spread to vital organs. Some 50,000 new cases are reported each year, along with 5,000 fatalities. Lupus is an example of another type of immune problem, an autoimmune disease. This is, in effect, civil war in the body. In such a disorder, something goes awry in the immune system, and the T-cells turn against the normal cells of their own body, treating them as "not self." In lupus, investigators believe, the problem may be a lack of suppressor T-cells, which causes runaway antibody production, thus creating antibodies against a patient's own normal tissues and organs. Not only lupus but some forms of anemia, rheumatoid arthritis, hepatitis, rheumatic heart disease, and infantile eczema are among these self-destructive diseases. Possibly even aging. Some scientists believe that the disease-fighting, thymus-spawned white cells mutate as the immune system declines with age and attack perfectly normal cells. The result of this internal warfare, it is theorized, is the deterioration and destruction of the body. For what goes on within your every cell affects you as a whole person.

The suggestion that autoimmunity is at the heart of aging is not a new one. The Russian biologist and Nobel laureate Elie Metchnikoff (1845–1916) was particularly interested in it — though he didn't call it that — and he convinced himself that if it could be dealt with, humans might well live to be 150. Metchnikoff discovered how bacteria are destroyed by the scavenger cells called phagocytes. Moreover, he extended that scavenger cell theory to an explanation of the aging process that is still considered a viable one by modern-day gerontologists. "Just as the pigment of the hair is destroyed by phagocytes," said Metchnikoff, "so also the atrophy of other organs of the body, in old age, is very frequently due to the action of devouring cells which I have called macrophages. These are the phagocytes that destroy the higher elements of the body, such as the nervous and muscular cells, and the cells of the liver and kidneys. . . . The bleaching of the hair and atrophy of the brain in old age furnish important arguments against the view that senescence is the result of arrest of the reproductive powers of the cells. Hairs grow old and become white without ceasing to grow. The cessation of the power of reproduction cannot be the cause of the senescence of brain cells for these cells do not reproduce even in youth."

In the case of cancer, long suspected of being an immunological disease, there is increasingly strong support for the theory that the body has its own efficient means of dealing with cancer cells, and that the malignancy arises as a result of a failure of certain immune processes. It is known, for instance, that the thymus-dependent immune system does not function well in Hodgkin's disease, a cancer of the lymph nodes and glands. (Lymph nodes, which filter impurities, contain tissue masses with spaces reserved for the production of disease-battling lymphocytes.) The link between aging and the development of cancer is an important one since with advancing age the T-cells — which fight invading antigens directly — lose their ability to proliferate as readily as in the young. They don't repair themselves as easily, either — which accounts for why your body doesn't repair a wound as speedily when you're older. Tired or defective, or both, the aging defense line just doesn't produce enough antibodies — or produce them fast enough — to deal with damaging outside agents that bring either disease or possibly even some of the traits of aging. The result is that the body is overwhelmed before it can marshal its protectors.

But, it may not be a no-win situation. Animal studies at Argonne National Laboratories, for example, have demonstrated that, while older animals normally produce fewer antibodies than do younger ones, with proper stimulation it is possible to raise the level of production in the older so that they end up with as many antibodies as are found in the young. By injecting old dogs with bacteriophage, a bacteria-killed virus, the researchers were able to get the animals to produce as much protective antibody as did younger animals also given the injection.

On another tack, Dr. Takashi Makinodan of the Gerontology Research Center removed white cells from young rats and injected them into older rats, boosting their resistance to disease and enabling them to withstand ordinarily fatal doses of disease-carrying bacteria. In other experiments, Dr. Makinodan found that by injecting spleen cells from younger mice, the life span of a mouse could be lengthened by nearly a third. The implications of all of this are that with proper stimulation and treatment, an older animal — and don't forget that the category includes us — can be made as resistant to certain types of disease as a younger one normally is, and that perhaps the immunity to disease can be improved in both groups. Says Dr. Makinodan: "We know that most people die of infection rather than senility or old age, and that when the immune system breaks down it affects so many other physiological functions. We feel that if we can prevent this, or reverse this decline, we may be able to lessen the severity of the ailment. Put another way, one has the suspicion that aging is caused by one or a few underlying mechanisms, and the reason we see all of the different kinds of declining physiological functions is a sort of domino effect. There must be just one or two things that trigger the whole event, and I think that the immune system could be one of these. We're very excited about it, and we're banking on the immune system as a way to prevent going downhill."

Though it hasn't yet been tried on humans, the results of the various immune experiments suggest that one day disease-fighting cells might be removed from a person while that person is young and healthy, frozen at $-200°$ C., then injected back in later life. The result might be an older individual better able to withstand disease and the cellular deterioration that hastens the aging process. "The difficulty in doing the mouse immune work in humans is a logistical one," explains Dr. Makinodan. "The good cells are in your marrow, and marrow tap isn't that easy. It's an engineering problem, but it's not unsurmountable. We're hoping that we'll be able to translate some of this mouse work into primate studies, and in fact this is the whole approach with our new, younger scientists. They're still interested in basic research, but they would like to see it all translated. This is a different attitude from my time. Some of them, this new breed of scientist, are willing to move faster. In our time, we used to take it all very systematically, one step, two steps. But they take step one, and step two, and they say, let's forget steps three and four, let's take a chance and go right to five."

If the immune system could, indeed, be shored up or altered, it would become, as we have said, a more effective bulwark against an impressive litany of ailments, aging among them. Already, it has been demonstrated that the system can be goaded into destroying the cancers that threaten it. A few years ago, Dr. Edmund Klein of Roswell Park Memorial Institute in Buffalo and Dr. Isaac Djerassi of Mercy Catholic Medical Center in Philadelphia brought about dramatic improvement in a group of cancer patients by injecting them daily with massive doses of monocytes, a special type of white blood cell. Some investigators believe that monocytes are responsible for the destruction, under normal circumstances, of grafted organs and of cancer cells. Djerassi also developed a machine that can extract, over a four-hour period, billions of monocytes from healthy donors by trapping them on a nylon filter. Injected into fifteen patients with cancers that had spread from internal organs to the skin surface, the monocytes brought about either a decrease in size or complete disappearance of the surface cancers in all of the patients. And the monocytes did the job within hours or days. Continuing injections of the monocytes were necessary to prevent the tumors from recurring.

Much of the monocyte work, of course, is still merely a model to demonstrate a research principle, and the injections are not yet a practical treatment for cancer. In the aforementioned fifteen patients, for instance, it is not known whether the white cell therapy has any effect on the internal tumors that gave rise to the skin lesions. It is also not yet known whether the injected monocytes kill the cancer cells directly, or whether they trigger the production of new monocytes at the site of the cancer.

The thymus gland, with its crucial roles in both the immune and the endocrine systems, is also under the close scrutiny of the new gerontologists. It works full tilt during embryonic growth, setting up centers for the production of lymphocytes in the spleen and lymph nodes. But following puberty, it begins to shrink, nearly disappearing with adulthood. The gland's characteristic rapid cell turnover is of interest because, according to one current line of reasoning, organs with proliferating cells lose their function with age. It is known, for example, that surgical removal of the thymus gland results in lymphopenia, a reduction in the number of lymphocytes in circulating blood. Recently, Dr. Allan Goldstein and his research team at the University of Texas discovered that a decreased level of thymosin, a key hormone produced by the thymus, retards the immunological system. "We hope to find a way to increase a patient's immunological response to disease by manipulating the amount of thymosin in the blood," he says. "We know that the injection of mice with thymosin increases their immunity and resistance to disease, and we have good reason to suppose it will do the same in man."

As is the case in any science like gerontology that has as many theories as theorems, interpretations vary. While all who work in the field would agree that immunological defects are certainly more common among the elderly and do weaken the body's natural resistance to disease, several scientists question whether the fault lies with the age of the cells that make up the immune system. One of them is Dr. David E. Harrison of the Jackson Laboratory in Bar Harbor, Maine. Harrison believes, and his research has demonstrated, that the cells from the gland that touches off immune system activities may be able to live and perform normally far longer than expected. Experimenting with laboratory mice, Dr. Harrison focused on stem cells. These come from bone marrow before traveling to the thymus, where they gain their immunological capability. He removed these cells from both young and old donors, and then transplanted them into young animals which had been irradiated to destroy their own stem cells. Once inside, the transplanted cells went to work. The old ones worked as effectively as the cells from young donors in providing immune responses in the recipient animals. Harrison's research indicates that these particular cells are not programmed internally to lose their ability to function after a specified time. Thus, he reasons, most of the loss of the vital immune system in old age depends on other factors. Harrison's research ought to stimulate a reexamination of current theories of immunological decline in old age, and it also raises anew the question of what does cause aging if separate parts of the body are not timed internally to stop working. "As they grow older," Harrison suggests, "the separate parts of the body may interact less effectively with each other, although they are individually healthy, or nearly so. Those separate cells and tissues are so dependent on each other that defective interactions may well cause all of them to decline in functional ability."

Chapter Eight

NOT TOO LONG AGO, the repairman came to replace our washing machine. It was worn out and old, and the rubber hoses were stiff and cracked; the once soft fiber ring that cushioned the top as it slammed shut countless times was brittle and now broke easily into bits. I recall looking sympathetically at the old hose as it trailed through the house, still attached to the washer that was being trundled out to the van, and I shook my head sadly. When the man hooked up the new machine he snapped on some new hose, too, and it was flexible, eager, and it had that clean, sweet smell of good, real rubber. I looked at the hose, after the man had gone, and thought, We'll probably replace it again and again and again. But that's the way it is with rubber, and with leather, and that's the way it is with our skin and our blood vessels.

As we age, these things lose their elasticity. Even the membrane that lines the inside of our mouths becomes dry, wrinkled and cracked. Our aging stomachs, less re-silient than they were in our youth, take longer to heal when they are eaten into by the acids of emotional stress and the aspirin that eases the pain of aching joints, or the cancer causing and suspected cancer causing addi-tives in the food we eat and drink. One day we will all lose our elasticity for good and shrink down to nothing more than bones and leather, and after that into com-post. And therein lies the tale of another theory of aging. It begins with a form of duplicating machine that some of you may remember, the so-called hectograph. Years ago, before the days of Xerox and 3M copiers, I ran a hectograph, a Ditto, while working as an office boy. It was a small machine, about the size of today's desk-top electric copiers. You "loaded" it with a large roll of gelatin-coated fabric, much as one loads film in a cam-era, stretching the gelatin sheet across the machine and fixing the end into a slot on the opposite side. After pull-ing it tight and locking it into place, you typed your purple ink master. You pressed that down onto the gela-tin sheet, passed a roller over it and peeled off the mas-ter, leaving the reversed imprint on the gelatin. Then, all you had to do was lay a sheet of transfer paper on the gelatin imprint, run a roller over it and peel off a purple copy. You got a half dozen or so readable copies before it all started to fade away on the gelatin sheet. You also had to change the roll regularly because eventually it swelled up, then dried out and cracked.

It was tedious work and I hated it, and that gelatin sheet used to have an awful smell, especially in the summer. But, while I was complaining, an industrial chemist at Ditto, Inc., which made the hectograph "films," was taking a keener interest in the gelatin coating. Dr. Johan Bjorksten had been investigating ways to control the elasticity, temperature diffusion, and swelling characteristics of the gelatin. Then, suddenly, which is the way things often happen with scientists, it struck Bjorksten that there were marked similarities between the way the gelatin and human tissues behave during aging, and that the similarities had to be more than coincidental. He reasoned that the "aging" of hectographic duplication film, which is a protein substance, and the aging of the human body, also composed of protein, involve chemical reactions that lead to water loss and loss of elasticity. These "symptoms" also become evident as the process known as tanning occurs. Tanning is the stiffening of hide into leather by treatment with substances such as tannin, an extract of bark and several plants. The hardened, scabby appearance of wound tissue is another example of tannins at work, as is the bitter, dry taste of an unripe persimmon.

It all led Bjorksten to wonder not only whether aging of the human body is an instance of a progressive tanning reaction, but also whether by arresting the process, or delaying it, as the photographic and duplication industries have done by various means, life might also be prolonged. Eventually, he incorporated his speculations about aging into an intriguing theory that has come to be known as molecular cross-linking.

Molecules, as most of us know, are the smallest units into which a substance can be divided and still retain all the chemical identity of that substance. They are chemical combinations of two or more atoms, linked by their outer orbital electrons to form a specific chemical compound. So small are they that in one cubic centimeter of air in an ordinary room, there are 27×10^{18} of them — or the figure 27 followed by eighteen zeroes. There are more molecules in water than in air, and if they were stretched in a row, 300,000 of them would be required to reach the thickness of a sheet of paper in this book.

With time, goes the theory, chemical agents begin to gum up the works — in rubber hoses and human body alike — by forcing the molecules to cross-link, or glue together. This results in what we have described as tanning. In our bodies, for example, this tanning process affects the basic building material, collagen, that ubiquitous substance that gives us our elasticity. As the long fibers of collagen begin to form cross-links, they undergo a dramatic alteration, something like the vulcanization of rubber. In skin collagen, the change is quite noticeable — from softness and suppleness in infancy to the dry, inelastic skin of old age. This accumulation of burdensome molecules — a slow process that, the theory holds, is what brings on all of the manifestations of old age — has been described as a "frozen metabolic pool" that can eventually clog and destroy our cells.

The substances capable of cross-linking the body's molecules of protein are found in all living cells and in normal blood and serum. They include citric acid products that result when fat is broken down, and several metals that are able to combine with body-building, organic substances. They may also be stimulated to action by such outside agents as radiation. Human beings, says

Bjorksten, contain about twenty parts per million of substances capable of cross-linking. In a 70-kilogram (155 pound) person, this would mean 1.4 grams of cross-linkers. This number is enough to ensure that every theoretically possible type of cross-linkage will be found in the body a great many times, and this will lead to complexes of giant inert molecules that cannot be excreted. Gradually crowding out the cells' other constituents, these "agglomerates" bring about a continual decline in the cells' activity and ability to cope with stresses. In cases involving cell division, Bjorksten explains, timing of the cross-linking event is critical. If, for instance, a gene is dividing and the two halves are suddenly linked by a cross-linker that happens to float by and are unable to separate, the cell either dies or the cross-linkage ruptures the genetic molecule, causing a mutation. As our cells clog, stiffen, mutate, and lose their function, so, too, do our tissues and organs which are made up of those cells.

Bjorksten believes that there is ample evidence indicating that during the aging process large molecules undergo changes in a manner that can be explained only by his theory. In a pinheaded organism called *Tokophyra*, for example, a form of protein has been observed to pile up with age. Such pileups of protein-containing material have also been noticed in rat liver, in dog and human nerve cells, the eye lenses of rats, human heart muscle, and in collagen, which is, as we have said, the most common protein in our bodies.

Because the aging of skin is speeded up by exposure to ultraviolet light, which includes intense sunlight, Bjorksten and his colleagues have radiated gelatin cells to see if they, too, undergo similar changes. They do. The proof was cross-linkage in the gelatin.

Bjorksten, of course, points always to the loss of elasticity as one of the most striking effects of cross-linking, and as one of the most universally accepted indications of progressing age. Just as the cross braces in a bridge contribute to rigidity, he says, so, too, does a cross-link in tissue. The whole idea may be likened to men in a chain gang. Linked together, they may not be exactly crippled, but their capacity to work is certainly limited drastically. If some way could be found to break the links, Bjorksten believes, the bonds of aging might also be loosened. A dedicated and consistent chemist, Bjorksten no longer attempts to polish his theory. That, he feels, was shown long ago to be valid. Instead, he has devoted his energy to looking for chemical agents that can snap apart cross-linkages. Convinced as he is of cross-linking's role in the aging process, he contends that the only way to really control aging is to find the means to break down the cross-linked insoluble molecules in the cells, reducing them to excretable components. His work toward that end has resulted in some preliminary successes in animals. He has already prepared enzymes that are able to dissolve the supposedly insoluble components of human tissues, and injected these into mice, chiefly to determine toxicity. Thus far, there have been no positive conclusions — except, as Bjorksten says, "There are no apparent negative results."

The hunt for a proper anti-cross-linking enzyme is no wild goose chase. Various naturally occurring enzymes do, in fact, range through our bodies to split up any number of cross-linkages that take place. Some of the cross-linkages, however, are immune to the enzymes' catalytic action. The result, as we have seen, is an interweaving of more and more molecules which eventually takes its toll on many of the body's components and functions.

Interestingly, one possible source of an anti-cross-linking enzyme might be the soil. Bacteria in the earth carry those enzymes, and we know that they work because buried bodies eventually decompose. Thus, the enzymes of soil bacteria that thrive on the resilient, cross-linked material in cadavers may well be the key to breaking down these tough molecule structures. As one recent geriatric publication comments: "Experiments with enzymes of soil bacteria indicate that 'elixirs' capable of removing at least some of the inert molecular accretion in older systems may appear in the 1970s, almost certainly will be available in the following decade."

Whether any of this will lead to an enzyme-loaded antiaging pill that would unstick aged, joined molecules is pure speculation. Bjorksten worked for a time under a $250,000 grant from the Upjohn Company to develop such an enzyme product, but the grant was not renewed. The reason given by the pharmaceutical company was that at least ten years more and another $10 million would be needed to prove such a pill safe and effective to the FDA. It also sought to downplay the impression that a product capable of adding years to one's life and rejuvenating the entire aged population was just around the corner. Nevertheless, Upjohn commended Bjorksten

as a "very able and respected scientist" whose work has
added considerably to the understanding of cell metabolism.

There, for the moment, the cross-link theory of aging
lies, and the possibility of an immediate "youth pill" is
remote. Several scientists feel the theory has no merit,
that it is a result not a cause of aging, and that there is
no real evidence to show that age-associated cross-linkages actually occur inside cells. Collagen cross-linking,
some believe, is a normal maturing process that occurs
during growth and development but which does not continue into later life and become pathological. The process of aging, a lot of scientists are convinced, is genetically controlled, and collagen, though it is a factor, is not
the primary agent. Bjorksten, of course, feels that many
of the theories of aging either build on the cross-link
idea or are special instances of it. The various cellular
theories, for instance. Cell mutations, he says, which
bring forth less viable cells on continued division over
the years, are, as explained earlier, cross-linkage by a
roaming cross-linking agent that prevents the separation
of both chromosomes. The hormone theory, which
ascribes aging largely to hormone changes, he points out,
describes one of the mechanisms by which advancing
age effects are caused. "But then what causes the initial
fluctuations in hormones?" he asks. "We are again back
to the same cause. There is no known reaction other than
cross-linkage by which such a minute trace of active
substances actually known to be present in the body can
cause major damage to the active giant molecules." As
for another theory, that certain "age pigments" accumu-

late in many cells with increasing age, interfering with their function, Bjorksten says they have been shown to consist primarily of highly cross-linked proteins. These age pigments are tied also to a theory of aging dealing with so-called free radicals — which will be discussed in the following chapter and which, many scientists believe, is not incompatible with the cross-linkage theory. There is, additionally, the suggestion of several researchers that antibodies are cross-linking agents, and this, of course, relates the Bjorksten theory to immunology. Finally, with regard to a suggestion by Dr. Hans Selye, the noted authority on stress concepts, that aging may be attributed to the effects of calcium on the system, Bjorksten feels that this also ties neatly into the cross-link concept because the calcium ion is bivalent — that is, it has the combining power of two — and is, therefore, a potential cross-linking agent.

For the moment, as I said, Bjorksten is doing no more work to prove his theory since he believes that, while it no doubt will be polished and supplemented in future years, its essential elements will continue to stand the test of time. Rather, he is following the guidelines it has provided toward application. "When a physician is 99 percent certain his patient suffers from pneumonia," he says, "he will prescribe for pneumonia. He will not wait for the autopsy to be 100 percent certain of his diagnosis. We felt that way. Being confident that we are on the right track, we said, 'How can we do something about the aging per se?'"

Chapter Nine

NEWSPAPERS, WE ALL KNOW, yellow and grow brittle with age. This happens because paper is cellulose, a carbohydrate. As it combines with the oxygen in the air through exposure to it, the carbon and hydrogen that make it a carbohydrate "burn" ever so slowly. This is a process barely noticeable, but it is going on, no mistake about it. Scientists refer to the conversion as oxidation, a reaction in which oxygen alters the makeup and function of a molecule. In chemistry, oxidation is a term used to express any reaction involving direct combination of an element or compound with oxygen. More precisely, however, it refers to a reaction in which an element or group of elements loses one or more electrons from the outer shell of each atom. The rusting of iron is an oxidation process in which iron, exposed to air in the presence of water, forms the familiar compound that coats it. When we burn coal in a furnace or gasoline in a car's engine, rapid oxidation is taking place, converting the carbon to carbon monoxide. Spread an oil-base paint on a wall and it will dry into a tough, thick skin. Oxidation. And in our bodies, the food we eat is also slowly burned, oxidized, for energy. Even on the vine, our fruits and vegetables are affected by the oxygen in the air. Enzymes in bananas, apples, peaches, pears and potatoes, cause the flesh and skin of these foods to darken when they are exposed to air after being cut, bruised or allowed to overmature. The chemical action responsible for this — it is form of oxidation — is known as enzymatic browning.

There is a clue here for gerontologists, in the yellowed newspaper, the dried paint, the rusted out piece of iron, and the blackened banana. And yet another theory of aging. Simply stated, it is that we are oxidizing in much the same way that all of the aforementioned do. The theory is the brainchild of Dr. Denham Harman of the University of Nebraska School of Medicine, and it centers on an erratic class of substances called free radicals. These are quite unstable fragments of molecules, or molecules missing an electron, that roam freely about after their breakup from the original, seeking a union with any new substance they can find. One gerontologist has compared them to convention delegates who have gotten away from their wives, looking to couple with anything that's loose in the vicinity. Free radicals are created by oxidative reactions, and it is their handiwork that dries the paint, stiffens rubber tires and tubes and hoses, spoils lard and butter (oxidation causes the development of rancid tastes and odors in foods that contain fats and oils), and thickens atmospheric pollutants into smog with the help of the sun's heat. At the core of a large body of natural and industrial decay processes, free radical reactions cause many of the undesirable cross-linkages, mentioned earlier, in our bodies as well as in rubber balls. They foul up our cells, scramble their genetic messages, injure the immune system, and according to the theory, they make us sick and they make us old. The theory's adherents believe that there is little difference in the degradative changes free radicals touch off, whether they are associated with bodily aging or with the decay of a commercial product. Free radicals and the oxidative reactions they are so closely linked to may be another sort of biological clock, one that regulates the rate at which we age by regulating the rate of bodily oxidation. And if so, if free radicals are clocks of a kind, they are vulnerable to tinkering. For, in the human body, there are appropriate levels of antioxidants, chemical scavengers that routinely mop up free radicals when the need arises. Antioxidants occur also in nature — one can, for example, prevent or delay enzymatic browning by dipping freshly cut fruits in orange, lemon or pineapple juices, which contain the antioxidants limonene and ascorbic acid. By boosting the levels of antioxidants in our bodies, some gerontologists suggest, aging might be postponed.

Before we talk about free radical suppression, however, let's look at how these fast-moving, short-lived, eager-to-recombine fragments are produced. There are, it turns out, many ways. One is when oxygen reacts in the body with polyunsaturated fats, the kinds found in margarines. The more such fat we consume, the more free radicals are formed because the fat steps up the cells' oxidation mechanism. Free radicals are also formed by radiation, and when they are created in this manner they become extremely potent cross-linking agents. (To add strength to his own theory, Johan Bjorksten has pointed out that commercial polymers — compounds of high molecular weight — are made more temperature resistant with radiation.) On a vaster scale, radiation-born free radicals doubtless played an important part billions of years ago in the formation of life out of the primordial atmosphere. Bathed continually in the ionizing radiation of the sun, the vital constituents of the early atmosphere — methane, ammonia and water vapor — oxidized into oxygen, nitrogen, and carbon dioxide. Swarms of free radicals were created, more powerful cross-linking agents than the radiation-formed radicals that tie polymers together. Out of it all emerged the sophisticated amino acids, the units out of which protein, the chief component of life, is made.

But, while free radicals were prime movers in such a high calling as life's creation, in our bodies they appear to be pests, seemingly negating all the good in which they once had a hand. They can disrupt the function of the cell membrane, that thin, pulsing, porous envelope that wraps the cell and holds it together like a sausage casing. Because the membrane (through which nutrients seep in and waste seeps out) is high in unsaturated fat, it is an excellent breeding ground for the free radicals. Once they get into the cell through the membrane, free radicals can damage the delicate organelles within. They interfere with the action of lysosomes, tiny bodies that use their digestive enzymes to process the raw materials such as fats and proteins that are necessary to sustain the cell. Interference with the cell's nutrients in this way means eventual cell death, and possibly the breakdown associated with aging. The nucleic acids — biochemicals that include DNA, the carrier of genetic information in the cells — are highly sensitive to an assault by free radicals. Under attack by hordes of free radicals, these vital acids may be so affected that the replicating process of the cell, essential for growth and development, is blocked or slowed. Errors may be made by the cells' message-system gone haywire, and all manner of nasty events take place. Collagen, the great stabilizer, deteriorates, as does elastin, another protein found in elastic tissue. Gooey deposits of all kinds of material begin to form. And among the more interesting of these is amyloid, a protein substance formed by free radical reaction and found in various tissues and organs, including the brain, in increasing amounts with age. Its presence in large amounts is called amyloidosis, a disease that holds special interest for those who study the biology of aging.

Known for about a century, amyloid is deposited in plaques, somewhat like the plaques that harden the body's arteries in atherosclerosis. These plaques are found not only in the brain but in the heart, liver and spleen, and are also common in aging geese, horses, bees, ostriches and primates. Amyloid deposits are widespread in elderly human beings, found, in fact, in ninety percent of people who live to be ninety. The deposits also turn up as a serious complication in disorders such as rheumatoid arthritis, leprosy, diabetes and tuberculosis. And while the evidence is not yet conclusive, there is a very strong suggestion that amyloid deposits so damage brain cells and brain blood vessels that senility, one of the major complications of aging, results. In 1964, in fact, Dr. Robert Terry of Albert Einstein Medical School discovered that the senile plaques he turned up in brains were made of amyloid. Moreover, by interfering with the way other cells in the body work, amyloid may also have much to do with aging in toto. "We cannot conclude that amyloid is a cause of abnormal behavior and senility," says Dr. Evan Calkins of State University of New York at Buffalo. "But it does seem to be a property of aging related to it. And since it occurs almost universally, it behooves us to look closely at it."

Thus far, there is no way to rid the system of unwanted amyloid — which would be a desirable end if, as some scientists believe, it is a true protein of aging, that is, one that actually helps bring on some of the degenerative changes of age. Dr. John Wright of Johns Hopkins School of Medicine has dissolved amyloid deposits in a test tube by treating them with the enzyme trypsin. The enzyme has also been used to dissolve some amyloid deposits that occur in the body, but it appears to be ineffective against deposits associated with senility. Wright found, for example, that the enzyme helped eliminate amyloid deposits in kidney and liver cells from a fifty-one-year-old man. But an eighty-seven-year-old senile man's cells were resistant to the trypsin treatment.

Another form of deposit associated with senescence and born of free radical reaction is lipofuscin. It is often referred to as "age pigment" and it takes the form of yellowish-brown clinkers. Not the same material that appears on your skin as so-called age spots, nor the same as amyloid, lipofuscin accumulates in cells when free radicals react with unsaturated fats. This buildup in the cells is as detrimental to smooth performance as is sugar in the gas tank of an automobile. Though a number of scientists do not believe that such pigments are harmful, suggesting that they are not a cause but a product of aging, there have been reports as far back as 1894 of pigment deposits in the cytoplasm of nerve cells of senile individuals. Recent studies with mice have shown that the frequency of cell-bearing lipofuscin granules as well as the number of granules per cell increases with age. And at a 1971 Zurich forum on aging, Dr. Charles G. Kormendy, a researcher at Bristol Laboratories, pointed out that several rare diseases show heavy deposits of lipofuscin in the brain and that these are accompanied by serious mental impairment. "Although we have no proof that lipofuscin de facto interferes with normal cellular function," he said, "its preponderance during aging, particularly in the neurons of the brain and in the heart muscle, could hardly be regarded as inconsequential." *Medical World News*, in a special report on aging that same year, noted that at least three drugs reportedly disrupt lipofuscin deposition, two of which have also been used to restore learning behavior in rats with induced brain disease. Experiments with a highly promising drug, centrophenoxine, have been under way for some time at Emory University by Kalindas Nandy, an associate professor of anatomy. Nandy has been studying the distribution of lipofuscin in various tissues, concentrating mainly on the brains of aging animals. Not only does the drug appear to slow down the rate of lipofuscin formation, but it has even extended the life of some species of animals and insects.

Centrophenoxine first raised scientific interest in 1959 with the report of a French botanist, G. Thuillier. He told how, in frustration over some laboratory incident, he threw a batch of the chemical out the window. A withering, yellow-leafed plant underneath caught the solution and in a short time turned a healthy green. Nandy has experimented with centrophenoxine in guinea pigs and mice, and his results have been most heartening. In one test, he and a colleague injected it into aged guinea pigs and found that the lipofuscin deposits in their nerve cells began to shrink until finally about ninety-five percent had vanished. Some of the animals were as old as six years, which is roughly equivalent to ninety in humans, and when put into cages they behaved lazily, refusing to move even for food. Centrophenoxine injections not only cut back the deposits of age pigment but made the animals more active and alert, and improved their appetite. Turning his attention to mice, which have a shorter life span than guinea pigs, Nandy gave them the drug, cut down the rate of lipofuscin formation in their brains and nerve cells, and even wiped away some of the deposits already present. The injections also lengthened the animals' life spans by about twenty percent. Untreated mice live about two years, but most of the animals treated with centrophenoxine reached thirty months. One group, in fact, contained twenty which lived to be thirty-six months, the equivalent of about one hundred years in humans. The treated mice, like the guinea pigs, were more alert, active and slimmer, the hair of the older ones even grew back, and psychological maze-testing demonstrated a significant improvement in learning and memory. Other researchers have given the drug to flies and increased their life spans by almost thirty percent.

Although centrophenoxine has been widely studied in animals, it is not available for use in human patients in the United States. It has, however, been tried in humans in France, West Germany, Sweden and Denmark, and reportedly has helped in treating senility. Thus far, though, there has been no indication that it prolongs the life span of human patients.

In addition to depositing lipofuscin and amyloid in our hidden innards, gumming up our cells, doing all kinds of aging damage and maybe even regulating the speed at which we age, free radical reactions may also promote abnormal growths, such as tumors. And here it is the polyunsaturated fats that may be at fault. As noted earlier, when oxygen reacts in the body with these fats, oxidation is boosted and so is the number of injurious free radicals. Several studies show a higher incidence of cancer where diets high in polyunsaturates and low in saturated fats are eaten. (Polyunsaturated fats, as every dieter knows, are found in substances derived from vegetables, such as corn oil margarine and safflower oil. Saturated fats are found in animal derived foods, such as beef, cream and butter.) Recently, scientists at Boston University School of Medicine fed rats both kinds of diet, then gave them cancer-inducing chemicals. The animals fed the diet high in polyunsaturated fats developed more large bowel cancers than those fed saturated fats. Another study reported a correlation between soft, oily ear wax — which may be caused by increased consumption of polyunsaturates — and increased incidence of cancer. People with dry ear wax were found to have fewer cancers.

As Dr. Selwyn A. Broitman, a professor of microbiology at Boston University, has pointed out, "Extrapolating from animal to human studies always entails some difficulties, but the findings would suggest that diets high in polyunsaturated fats aimed at reducing cholesterol levels in the blood might conceivably increase the risk of developing cancer of the large bowel." The irony here, of course, is that millions of people have forsaken high saturated fat diets for diets heavier in polyunsaturates because of the evidence that heart disease is associated with animal fats. While we may well ward off atherosclerosis by substituting polyunsaturates for all that butter — and that concept is now being challenged for other reasons — there is a good possibility that we may be doing ourselves just as much harm. Before you drastically alter your diet, however, it would be wise to remember that the incidence of colon cancer is smaller than the incidence of heart disease, and that cutting polyunsaturates completely out of a diet would be folly since they are necessary for proper nutrition. Most researchers would agree with that. Nevertheless, some gerontologists think that, cancer aside, we may well be hastening our own aging by loading up on polyunsaturates and thereby getting all those free radicals to emerge from the stepped up cellular oxidation that comes with eating that sort of fat. Nebraska's Denham Harman, for one, has studied the effects of an unsaturated fat diet on the life span of rodents. He fed mice and rats, throughout their lives, diets composed of five, ten and twenty percent of lard, olive oil, corn oil, safflower oil and menhaden oil. One result of the study was that increasing the amount and/or degree of unsaturation of the dietary fat *decreased* the mean life span of the animals to as much as ten percent below that for those on the five percent lard diet, a diet least amenable to oxidative reactions. It would appear that as nauseating as a slab of lard on our dinner plates may seem to some, it might, after all, be of some benefit in our diet. Take blood pressure, for example. Harman says that the normal rise with increasing age — 103/70 at age ten as opposed, say, to 135/89 at age sixty — may be partly the result of oxidative reactions going on in the body. To back up that statement, he points to studies that have found a lower blood pressure in rats fed a lard diet than in those fed unsaturates. Likewise, the blood pressure of chickens maintained for three years on diets of ten percent of either corn oil or animal fat tended to be lower in the fowl receiving the animal fat. Dr. Edward R. Pinckney, a California physician who has written extensively on the potential toxicity of excessive polyunsaturates, cites a Los Angeles study done to determine if there might be some clinical association between a diet high in the polys and outward signs of tissue damage. Patients who visited a plastic surgeon's office were evaluated for signs of premature aging and were asked, at the same time, to complete a questionnaire designed to solicit information about their daily intake of fats. Of those evaluated, according to Pinckney, fifty-four percent stated and showed by the foods they listed that they ate more than ten percent polyunsaturates — that is, used only "special" margarines and polyunsaturated oils, and deliberately increased their consumption of fish. Furthermore, of those who deliberately forced polyunsaturates, seventy-eight percent showed marked clinical signs of premature aging. They also looked a good deal older than their chronological age. In this same group, according to Pinckney, sixty percent reported they had had at least one or more skin lesions removed because of suspected malignancy — after they had altered their dietary fat. In contrast, of those who did not go out of their way to eat polyunsaturates, only eighteen percent had any visible signs of premature aging, and only eight percent reported the removal of any precancerous skin lesions. In light of these findings, Pinckney feels that patients ought not go overboard on polyunsaturates in spite of the constant commercial and health agency pressure that is brought on them.

Fats in our diet are not the only problem. Trace metals, such as copper, are also implicated in the oxidation and free radical brew. Copper is an important ingredient in biological systems. Excess amounts, of course, are toxic, but we need it to the tune of two milligrams a day. Most of it is in the liver and bones, and it is essential to the synthesis of hemoglobin, the pigment in red blood cells that carries oxygen to our tissues. Animals on a low copper diet grow anemic, and without the metal even lower plant forms such as algae and fungi would not grow and reproduce. Copper, it turns out, serves as an effective catalyst in getting oxygen to react with various organic compounds. The free radicals generated when copper is the trigger have, in fact, been implicated in the development of atherosclerosis. When pigs are fed diets containing copper acetate, their aortic and coronary arteries clog up with the classic deposits that come with the artery-hardening disease. It is believed that the free radicals generated when copper intake is increased irritate fats found in the blood serum and in arterial walls. The reaction produces substances in amounts large enough to plug arteries. Researchers have also found that serum copper levels are significantly higher in persons with a history of myocardial infarction, which is damage to the heart muscle due to poor blood supply. Support for the idea that free radical action in vessel wall fats touches off harmful substances comes from studies of the water we drink. It has long been known that the mortality rate from coronary artery disease rises according to the softness of the water. This is probably due to the fact that copper levels in drinking water increase with softness. Higher blood copper levels trigger oxidation, then free radical production, then tissue irritants. "It is pertinent," says Harman, "that metropolitan areas of the U.S. with elevated rates for coronary heart disease also have elevated concentrations of copper in the drinking water."

In view of the evidence connecting free radical production to life-shortening and debilitating disease — possibly even to life span itself — scientists are considering ways to halt overproduction of these errant molecular fragments. We could, of course, be careful of our intake of copper and polyunsaturates — which would mean drinking unpalatable hard water instead of soft, and using animal fats instead of margarine and corn oil. Better yet, however, would be some ingredient, possibly an additive to our daily diets, that would cut the level of free radical reactions. If we could do this, say some researchers, the rate at which we degrade biologically would be slowed, and we would all win extra years of useful, healthy life. Enter a class of substances called antioxidants which inhibit free radical reactions. Chemical scavengers, we have called them, substances that stop butter from spoiling and rubber tires from rotting. Vitamin E is probably the best known of the antioxidants. The others have tongue-twisting names: 2-mercaptoethylamine, a radiation protector; a quinoline derivative used in animal feeds, known as athoxyquine; butylated hydroxytoluene, or BHT; and butylated hydroxyanisole, known more familiarly as BHA. The last two are usually listed on the backs of cereal boxes ("to preserve freshness") or on packages of processed foods that contain fat, such as cake mixes with shortening. BHA, for instance, has been added to foods since 1940 in rigidly controlled amounts. Without it, packaged foods such as breakfast cereals would have a shelf life of only four months. With it, life of the product is extended to one year.

Several antioxidants have been tested by being added to the daily diets of animals just before weaning. Some of the results have been startling, more so when one considers that humans might one day benefit. In Denham Harman's experiments, cancer-prone mice were used because their average and maximum life spans are relatively short. Although these animals usually die of such malignancies as lymphatic leukemia and breast cancer, they are suitable for such testing of the suspected influence of free radicals on aging because, if the theory is correct, the average age at which the disease appears might be increased. Every day, Harman fed his mice a commercial mouse diet containing an antioxidant — either 2-MEA, BHT or ethoxyquine — or no additives at all. What resulted was a significant increase in the average life spans of the mice fed diets laced with antioxidants. In some cases, Harman has succeeded in increasing the mean life span of his mice by twenty-five to fifty percent. The precise mechanism by which the antioxidants affected longevity — whether by inhibiting the cancers to which the mice were prone, or by preventing the formation of amyloid deposits — is not known. But the most reasonable explanation, Harman feels, is that the effect on longevity is the result of the inhibition of injurious free radical reactions originating within the animals' bodies. In light of his mouse data, Harman suggests that adding antioxidants to a properly selected natural diet may increase the average age at death of humans by ten percent or more. Also, the increase in duration of useful life would probably be greater, the younger the person when the treatment was begun. This does not mean, says Harman, that giving antioxidants to older persons will do no good. Conceivably, such treatment could have some benefit because the rate of aging seems to increase with age — an effect that may in part reflect a stepped-up attack on the body by free radicals as we grow older. In support of this notion is the fact that the serum level of copper — a free radical producer, you will recall — increases with age. Also, body levels of mercaptans, substances that inhibit free radical reactions, decrease.

Turning to vitamin E, or alpha-tocopherol as it is known chemically, it is not yet certain — despite some compelling laboratory evidence — that increasing the daily intake of this antioxidant will have any positive effect on longevity. A fat-soluble chemical, vitamin E is found naturally in vegetable oils, whole grains and even in fish, meats, eggs and green leafy vegetables. It is, as most of us know, a staple of vitamin enthusiasts who claim it can cure everything that ails us — aging, heart attacks, impotence, and cancer, to name but a few. A few years ago, however, a committee of the National Academy of Sciences charged that the various claims were misleading and without any solid experimental or clinical backing. Noting that the usual balanced diet supplies adequate amounts of the vitamin, the committee said supplements of it were unnecessary and that self-medication with vitamin E in the hope that a more or less serious condition would be alleviated "may indeed be hazardous, especially when appropriate diagnosis and treatment may thereby be delayed or avoided." Some people take 400 to 1,000 International Units a day, when only 30 are recommended by the FDA.

Despite the academy's caveat (and the efficacy overkill of the vitamin devotees), it would seem that sensible doses of the antioxidant every day have no harmful effect, and may even do some good. Dr. Henry Dymsza, a nutrition scientist at the University of Rhode Island, fed rats vitamin E and reported that there were no adverse results except at dosage levels of 1,000 times the daily requirement. The animals got 25, 50 and 1,000 times the norm, and after eight weeks those on the highest dose had significantly lower feed and protein deficiencies. When the animals were mated, fertility and survival of pups to weanlings had not been affected by the diets. But the number of pups born alive was significantly reduced in the 1,000-times group. Says Dymsza: "Vitamin E is a most interesting vitamin. When added to a tissue culture, its anti-oxidant characteristic has the ability to prolong the life of the culture. But in tests done earlier at URI, megadoses of the vitamin did not reverse or reduce senility in a group of elderly human subjects. It did not harm them, either. Whether it can prevent senility if started early enough remains to be seen. Scientists have not yet been able to say definitely that it benefits man beyond the normal required dose, but if taken in sensible larger doses it does not seem to be harmful."

In other URI work, rats were artificially aged by making them deficient in the vitamin. This response was based on earlier studies that determined that depriving animals of the vitamin produces an accumulation of age pigment in the brain and other organs, resembling pigment found in aged humans. In their research, the URI scientists set out to find whether the deficient rats would become senile like actual aged rats. To do this, they divided the rats into two groups, fed one normally for fourteen months and the other a vitamin E deficient diet. Both groups were put through a series of tests to see how well they could learn and remember. A third group of younger rats was also given the tests to determine whether they would do better than their older cousins. In one of the tests, the animals were placed in a special cage with an electrified floor. They heard a buzzer and ten seconds later received a mild but unpleasant shock. Eventually, the rats learned that they had to jump out of the cage as soon as they heard the buzzer if they were to avoid this shock. The slower they learned, the scientists reasoned, the more senile their brains. After five days, the researchers tested the rats to see how well they had learned their lessons. Other tests determined how well the older, younger, and vitamin-deficient rats could remember a one-time experience and a long-term task. The vitamin E deficient rats, it turned out, clearly did worse than the other rats their age. The younger rats did better than both the older and the deficient ones. The researchers also discovered that the deficient rats' brains had decreased in weight more than the others, just as occurs in humans who are senile.

In another test of vitamin E's capabilities — to determine whether it could decrease tumor incidence in animals by decreasing the level of free radical reactions — Harman fed rats diets containing safflower oil as the sole source of fat, with and without vitamin E. He found that addition of the vitamin decreased the incidence of gross tumors in female rats; and in some of the rats that did develop tumors, the ones fed the vitamin developed them at a later age than those "unprotected" by the antioxidant.

Other studies of vitamin E have found that it has a modest beneficial effect on the life span of rodents, certain worms and flies. Such results have prompted scientists to look into whether the vitamin can do the same thing in humans. But since testing the effects of any anti-aging additive on humans requires years, the studies have been done with human cells in test tubes. In one notable test in 1974, Drs. Lester Packer of the University of California and James R. Smith of the Veterans Administration Hospital in Martiniz, California, added vitamin E to human lung cells in a test tube. The cells kept dividing without sign of quitting, going well beyond the usual life span of such cells. However, in 1977, the two scientists reported that they repeated their experiment nearly a score of times and had not been able to duplicate the results of the first test. Moreover, neither have other investigators. The two scientists speculate that some special ingredient or ingredients in the serum they used to culture the first batch of cells did the trick. This is quite possible since each batch of a serum sold by biochemical firms is different in some slight way. If they are right, then it would appear that it is not just the addition of vitamin E that extends cell life, since it did not do so in other experiments. But it might have been the interaction of the vitamin with some other, unidentified substance in the growth serum. Packer and Smith have analyzed what original serum they had left, but have not been able to isolate anything that looks responsible. The other possibility is that their first experiment was a fluke, and that all of the others were correct.

Johan Bjorksten is among those convinced that vitamin E has a place in the quest for longevity, primarily through the antioxidant's effects on the circulatory system. But he feels strongly that the long-term, major breakthrough in the preservation of vitality can only come by utilizing enzymes to break the backbones between molecules, the cross-linking agents he believes are formed in advancing years by the oxidative and free radical reactions. "What can be hoped for of any vitamin therapy is only a delaying action," he says. "This, however, may be applicable now, and may give some of us the added years necessary to complete the larger and infinitely more tedious task of following the enzyme route to a happy conclusion." He points out that in small mammals, the addition of large amounts of vitamin E beyond generally adequate rations affects life expectancy unfavorably, when at all. "On long-lived organisms, such as humans, the preserving effect of vitamin E becomes more noticeable. On the basis of test results, an increase in life expectancy in the order of about three to five years and possibly up to ten to fifteen years in individual instances might be attainable by optimizing the supply of vitamin E. A major part of this increase will be due to increased protection of the circulatory system."

Harman's position is that he doesn't know whether vitamin E will have a beneficial effect on the aging process per se. But it might. He has suggested that free radicals are formed in the tiny powerhouses of the cells, the mitochondria. These organelles, he believes, are the biological clocks that regulate the rate of aging in mammals and possibly also in lower organisms. He bases this on the fact that over ninety percent of the oxygen consumed by mammals is utilized in the mitochondria, making them the site of oxidative reactions that occur at a continuous, high rate. When such reactions take place in, say, the mitochondria in muscle, collagen and elastin may deteriorate, resulting in the loss of elasticity seen in the elderly. "The correlation of degenerative diseases with aging," says Harman, "could be related at least in part to the concentration of molecular oxygen in the tissues of the body." Also, how long a mammal lives may have a good deal to do with how fast, how slow or how well its cells and tissues use oxygen. The rate at which that oxygen is utilized determines the severity of the damage produced by free radical reactions in the mitochondria — the amount of damage increasing with the amount of oxygen consumed. Death ultimately results. Small animals, for instance, generally have high metabolic action and shorter life spans.

If Harman's suggestion that the mitochondria are biological clocks is correct, then attempts to extend the human maximum life span by getting at free radical production at those sites may not be far off the mark. And vitamin E could conceivably do it. In any event, Harman suspects that the vitamin may at least decrease the incidence of cardiovascular disease and cancer. In view of the experiments with dietary fats and free radical inhibitors, he does feel it is reasonable to expect that cutting down on substances that increase free radical action, and adding antioxidants to a proper, natural diet, will result in an increase in the useful human life span. He suggests about 300 to 500 milligrams of vitamin E a week. How much it might help is difficult to say. Five, ten, fifteen years of healthier life is not without reason. Says Harman: "Following the dictum 'Do no harm,' some alterations could be made now in human diets along the lines indicated."

Chapter Ten

Some years before birth, advertise for a couple of
parents belonging to long-lived families.
— Oliver Wendell Holmes, Sr.

THROUGHOUT THIS BOOK, I have alluded often to biological clocks of aging, clocks that control our life spans. As
we have seen, they may be located in the hypothalamus,
ticking away our days through the nervous and endocrine systems. Or they may be in the energy-producing
mitochondria in every cell, pushing out free radicals, as
Denham Harman suggests. We cannot ignore the fact,
barring premature death by some nongenetic force, that
there are different life spans between and within species
of animals. And that alone is the best evidence in favor
of a clock somewhere inside everything that lives, plant
or animal, a timepiece preset by some chemical com-
mand at birth. It governs the many changes that occur in
our cells as we age, changes that presumably parallel the
aging process within the entire organism.

The theory that there is such a clock of aging in every cell is a fascinating one that many scientists view as the mainspring — continuing the metaphor — of gerontological research. I have chosen to include a discussion of it here, at the conclusion of our examination of the various theories of aging, because the cellular clock is an end in its own right. And this end has a good deal to do with how I perceive the story of aging research — as a story replete with theories but with a climax of its own, like any story, a high point of intensity beyond which we cannot go.

We have already had ample evidence that many aspects of bodily aging are linked to biochemical reactions. For just as a peach or banana darkens and spoils when it overmatures and oxidizes, so, too, in a sense, do we when the biochemical reactions of oxidation, cross-linkage, hormone secretion, and antibody-antigen are set off. But no matter how compelling all of the aforementioned theories of aging may sound, no matter how strongly we are tempted to choose one over the other and say that's what causes us to grow old and die and this is what we can do about it, the fact is that ultimately each and every one of the theories of aging must fall back on the cell, the smallest basic unit of life, and all of the delicate machinery it contains. If there is any single theory of aging — or, more accurately, any unifying theory of aging — it is the cellular. For cells do more than carry oxygen and carbon dioxide, and messages to the brain. They make protein, the stuff of which we are constructed, and they band together to perform special tasks, forming organs and tissues and whole human beings. When they quit making all this protein, we fall apart, pure and simple. Cells make the hormones and enzymes that keep us going, they divide and redivide to produce identical copies of themselves, over and over again. Thousands of new skin cells, for example, may be formed every day to replace those damaged or destroyed by injuries or disease; red blood cells and epithelial cells — those that line the intestines — are renewed in a few days or months. Heart and limb muscle cells renew at a slower pace, while liver cells hardly ever divide unless a portion of the organ is removed. Other cells, such as those in the brain and the rest of the nervous system, do not appear to be able to reproduce themselves, and even though these begin to die at the startling rate of some hundred thousand a day in our late twenties, there are billions in every one of us from birth, and we apparently withstand the depletion rather well.

But at some point, the process slows down and quits, and the cells die. At different rates, but they do die. Without them, alive and pulsing and replicating, there can be no life for the body's bones, flesh, blood and all the rest of it. Eventually, we age and die, and says one cellular theory, we do so according to some program, a time clock, built into each cell in every species that walks and crawls, grows, and swims on this earth. In 1961, an American biologist named Leonard Hayflick came up with the best evidence yet in support of such a genetic clock — not just a single clock in the brain that regulates the aging and death of every cell but one in each individual cell. In so doing he generally laid to rest the prevalent notion that cells in tissue culture are ageless, that they could, in effect, live forever if "fed" properly. Hayflick, then at the Wistar Institute in Philadelphia, removed soft, fibrous cells called fibroblasts from the lung tissue of a four-month-old human embryo. He cultured them and discovered that they doubled about fifty times, then stopped. Cells taken from the lung tissue of a twenty-year-old man, on the other hand, multiplied about twenty times before they slowed down and died. Next, Hayflick decided to find out whether the fibroblasts had a memory, that is, whether they could "recall" the number of times they had doubled. He froze some of his cell colonies in liquid nitrogen at different stages — after, say, ten or twenty doublings — thus stopping their "biological clocks" and the divisions. Amazingly, when the fibroblasts thawed they resumed dividing — with each taking up exactly where it had left off, multiplying only as many times as remained from their original program. For example, cells that had been frozen and stored at the twentieth doubling went on to divide about thirty more times before they quit at fifty. Further, the cells "remembered" the doubling level they had reached before storage even after a deep freeze that lasted for up to ten years.

Hayflick also found that the number of cell doublings is related to the life span of the species. Mouse cells, for instance, divide about twelve times, while those from a chicken, which lives many years more than a mouse, divide around twenty-five times. Long-living tortoises have cells that divide up to one hundred and twenty-five times. The number of doublings is also generally related to the age of the cell donor, with a decrease in the divisions the older the donor. Interestingly, in the premature aging disease known as progeria, when cells are removed from affected children — who have all the symptoms of age far beyond their time — and cultured, they double only a few times before fading out, just as occurs in the very elderly. (We'll come back to progeria later.)

Scientists were not always certain, however, that there was a limit to the doublings. For years, in fact, they had thought cells were immortal. If, as I said earlier, they could be "fed" properly, they could go on forever, went this line of reasoning. Among those convinced that cultured cells could, indeed, multiply ad infinitum was the noted French surgeon, experimental biologist and 1912 Nobel Prize winner, Alexis Carrel, who was instrumental in developing, among other techniques, a method for suturing blood vessels, and who pioneered in organ transplants and safe blood transfusions. Carrel apparently managed to keep chicken fibroblasts in culture continually growing and multiplying for nearly thirty-five years by feeding them a chicken embryo extract. He intentionally ended his experiment in 1939, calculating that if he had not destroyed some of his growing culture each day, it would have engulfed the earth's surface in twenty years.

In Germany, meanwhile, another researcher, Paul Ehrlich, started a culture of tumor cells from a mouse, cells that thrive today in laboratories throughout the world, seemingly immortal. That culture was begun in 1907. But the classic example of a long-thriving human cell line had its beginning in 1951 with cells obtained by Dr. George O. Gey, of the Johns Hopkins School of Medicine, from the cervix of a young woman with cancer. The woman, who eventually died of the malignancy, was known pseudonymously as Helen Lane. The cells, which continue to grow and divide in many laboratories and are still used in numerous research projects, are known as the HeLa Strain. The first human cancer cells to multiply in culture, HeLa cells have proved to be one of the hardiest and most studied human strains, having won immortality, of a sort, that escaped their original host.

If one takes Carrel's results — along with Ehrlich's and the amazing HeLa Strain — at face value, it is easy to conclude that the cell has nothing to do with biological aging since it seems to have this capacity for immortality. Aging, it could then be surmised, is a characteristic of the whole animal, not simply one of its parts, and is thus the result of complex changes occurring at a higher level than the cell. This, however, is now questioned by those who, like Hayflick, lean toward the idea of a cellular time clock of aging. Hayflick has suggested that every time Carrel fed chicken embryo extract to his "immortal" culture, the extract contained fresh, living cells, and this was the reason the cultures grew as they did for so many years. It has been suggested further that the reason the other long-lived cell lines — such as those from Ehrlich's mouse and Helen Lane — have continued to replicate indefinitely was because they were abnormal to begin with, that is, cancerous. Normally, cells have 46 chromosomes, 23 from each parent. The HeLa cells, however, were found to contain from 50 to 350. The malignancy, this line of reasoning holds, halts the biological clock of aging at the same time it drastically alters the mechanism that directs normal cell growth. It is another one of those bits of scientific irony. The cells attain immortality, but the price is a fatal disease for their owner.

It is widely believed that Hayflick's limit — as it is known — can be applied to other body cells besides the fibroblasts, and that the observations of events that transpire in laboratory culture dishes *do* have counterparts inside our bodies. Even though carefully cultivated laboratory fibroblasts manage their fifty doublings in about six months — compared to the many years required within the human body if all goes well — many believe that the limit holds, in the laboratory or in the body, and that human beings are programmed to live no longer than the uppermost limit of the species. Those fifty cell divisions that human cells undergo actually take approximately 115 years to complete — roughly the maximum life span we can expect under optimum conditions. The more of those conditions that are met, of course, the better the chances of our cells living out the maximum number of doublings. One condition might be that we come from a long-lived family strain. All of us know of, or belong to, families with ninety-year-old grandparents, or other long-lived members. Those extended years could be programmed into cells at some point — just as eye and hair color are — to show up in current or future generations; or, since we know that hundreds of diseases and defects arise either through direct inheritance or through inherited predisposition to one of them, life spans in families might well be dependent enough on that aspect of genetics so that the optimum number of doublings is not achieved. For example, although there is no evidence that heart attacks and stroke, or the atherosclerotic process that contributes to both diseases, are hereditary, a tendency toward these problems can definitely be inherited. Incidence is higher in some families than in others, and it is well known that if either of your parents has heart disease your chances of developing it are greater. Scientists also know that identical twins — those that develop from one egg — have a similar life span more often than fraternal twins, those which develop from two eggs fertilized by separate sperm. Furthermore, identical twins appear to die of the same causes more than twice as often as do fraternal twins. At UCLA, researchers found that in 2,000 sets of twins over age sixty, the identical twins had markedly more similar life spans than did the nonidentical. Again, the handiwork of genetics in longevity control.

Finally, there is the fact that women live longer than men — with the rule of female superiority in this regard applying also to zoo animals, spiders, fruit flies and chickens. However, there does not seem to be a direct effect of any harmful sex-linked genes in this. Rather, geneticists believe, males are less equipped genetically than women; they have enough differences in behavior, rate of metabolism and bodily structure to make them more vulnerable to disease and defects in prenatal, postnatal and adult life.

But despite the strong evidence in favor of a clock of aging, Hayflick doesn't believe we age simply because our cells quit dividing. First of all, he points out, humans

don't live long enough to enjoy a maximum number of
cell doublings. Second, he believes that it is the variety
of changes that take place *before* the cells lose their
capacity for division that are linked to the aging process.
"I think we have achieved in tissue culture what is
never, or only very rarely, achieved in the whole animal,"
he observes. "It may represent the ultimate limit that we
may perhaps someday achieve. What does us in now, as
far as clinical aging signs are concerned, I believe to be
those things that change in the cell during that period of
time prior to its loss of ability to divide, or to function.
It's those earliest events, say, 10, 15, 20 doublings before
the loss of division potential, that manifest themselves as
what we call age changes. So you're done in by them
well before your cells have stopped dividing."

But what is it that causes the cells to run out of power
so that they do not divide indefinitely? Before we attempt to answer that question, a review of some basic
cell biology and the mechanism of replication might be
helpful. The cell is a busy and highly organized entity.
Bacteria are made up of just one cell, the human body
consists of trillions, of different shapes and purposes for
being. Each cell is a teeming microworld full of the stuff
of life itself, a gelatinous place of perpetual motion held
together by the porous membrane that encases it. The
many components in every cell float about like wreckage
on a heaving sea. Indeed, each living human cell *is* a
miniature sea containing all of the salts found in the
oceans of earth, doubtless our inheritance from the days
when one of our fishlike ancestors mutated into a reptile
and crawled up onto the still-steaming land. Our analogy

to the ocean ends there, however. For though the cells' tiny bits and pieces appear to be drifting aimlessly, like so much flotsam, they actually are functioning in perfect harmony to carry out each cell's main occupation — the manufacture and use of vital proteins, both for itself and for other cells. Proteins, the reader will recall, are the familiar muscle-builders found in meat, fish, milk, cheese, eggs and beans. As we and other living things grow, we gain new cells, and proteins are essential for growth. (See Figure 1.) Without protein, our bodies would not make enough cells to maintain good health. But proteins are much more than simple body-builders. They are extremely complicated molecules made up of amino acids, and there are twenty different kinds. Hormones, as mentioned earlier, are proteins, and so are enzymes, those chemical workhorses that speed up the thousands of changes that take place regularly in our bodies. Other proteins are responsible for the actual structure of the cell's walls, and for such things as skin and hair.

Despite this wide variety of proteins, they all have one important factor in common — each is manufactured in the miniature chemical laboratory of the cell according to an exacting set of instructions sent out by the master molecule that carries genetic information, DNA (deoxyribonucleic acid). Let's look for it inside a typical cell, into the nucleus, the rounded control center that contains, among other elements, the threadlike chromosomes. Packed within these chromosomes, in sections — forty-six in the normal human cell, forty-two in white rats, fourteen in pea plants, eight in a fruit fly — are the genes, the units that make us what we are. Each of these tiny powerpacks is responsible for some characteristic — body build, eye color and temperament — and is about a hundredth the diameter of a human hair. Each gene, in turn, is made up of very long, slender molecules of two-stranded DNA twisted together and wound around an inner core of protein. (See Figure 2.) Every human cell has twenty-three pairs of DNA strands to coincide with the number of chromosomes from each parent. If we could stretch out a single cell's DNA molecules, they would reach for several feet, many thousands of times the width of the cell itself. A chemist looking closely at the composition of this twisted DNA ladder — the double helix, as it is known — would find no unfamiliar substances. They are all chemicals called nucleotides. The spiral sides of the ladder are phosphates, which are combinations of the mineral phosphorus, oxygen and sugars. The rungs are made of just four chemical molecules — adenine, guanine, cystosine and thymine (A, G, C, T). Each rung actually consists of two of the chemicals joined in the middle in a very precise way. For example, a half rung of C always joins with a half rung of G to form a whole rung; an A always ties into a T. But the possible arrangements of the steps are nearly endless. For instance, a set of steps, or rungs, might look like this: CG, GC, AT, TA, TA, AT, CG, CG, GC, AT, GC, AT, and so on. A virus might contain some 200,000 DNA rungs arranged in different sequences. A germ might have five or six million rungs in its chromosomes. (See Figure 3.) A single human cell, the top of the line of life, contains mind-boggling billions. What-

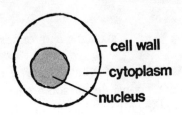

- cell wall
- cytoplasm
- nucleus

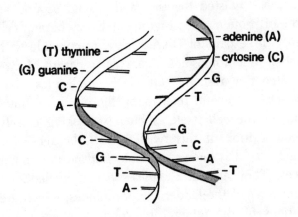

(T) thymine —
(G) guanine —
C —
A —
C —
G —
T —
A —

— adenine (A)
— cytosine (C)
— G
— T
— G
— C
— A
— T

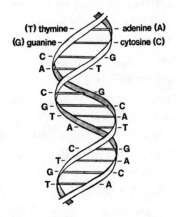

(T) thymine —
(G) guanine —
C —
A —
C —
G —
T —
A —
C —
T —
G —
T —

— adenine (A)
— cytosine (C)
— G
— T
— G
— C
— A
— T
— G
— A
— C
— A

ever the form of life, however — man, mouse or microbe — it is all composed of the same chemical ladder. It is only the *order* in which this four-letter chemical alphabet is arranged that spells out what form life will take, and gives each gene its own special code with which to direct the manufacture of the protein for which it is responsible. When you consider the thousands of proteins that go into a human body, each the handiwork of only one gene, you begin to get some idea of how busy a chemical factory a cell is.

Cellular action really begins when the DNA ladder unwinds and the rungs pull apart in the middle, a process that occurs every time a cell begins its ritual of dividing. All of the Cs unhook from the Gs, the Ts from the As. But soon, each freed side of the ladder and its half-rungs picks up new nucleotides that are always floating about in the cell. The Cs, Gs, Ts and As on the ladder halves link up with their proper floating partners, and new ladder sides are formed. Now where there was one twisted ladder there are two, identical in every way. Each new cell has its own DNA ladder in a new set of chromosomes, and each ladder comes fully equipped with the same coded genetic instructions that its parent has because its rungs are arranged in the same precise sequence. Each time a cell duplicates itself, so does its DNA.

The next step is for the cell to use the instructions coded in the genes. It does so in a manner somewhat like an architect passing blueprints to a construction engineer. The blueprints, in this case the genes, contain the coded instructions for making a specific protein. What

happens is this: a section of DNA, a gene, unzips itself
again and makes another nucleic acid called *messenger*
RNA, or mRNA. In doing so, the gene hands over to the
messenger the entire coded blueprint for one protein.
This done, it zips itself up once more. The messenger
now moves out of the nucleus into the cell's cytoplasm,
carrying the instructions to one of the dense granules,
called ribosomes, that lie scattered about. These are the
workshops where the proteins are assembled. At a ribo-
some, messenger RNA acts like a computer tape, running
out its coded message which contains a "grocery list" of
every amino acid needed to make the designated protein.
Another form of RNA now enters the picture. Called
transfer RNA, or tRNA, it takes the instructions and
floats out into the cytoplasm to hunt down the amino
acids called for in the code. After linking up with the
right amino acid, the transfer RNA takes it to the ribo-
some where, with the help of messenger RNA, a protein
with a special function is assembled.

Interestingly, while there are only twenty different
protein amino acids, they can be sequenced in a myriad
ways to build all of the protein required for a human
being.

Eventually, cells begin to take on special roles, duplicating at different rates and behaving in different ways.
One cell becomes a brain cell, another an eye cell, or a
bone cell, a liver cell, a skin cell. Why this all happens is
not fully understood. But scientists believe it has something to do with what they call the activator-repressor
mechanism. This amounts to a "switch" that turns certain genes on and off, deciding whether distinctive

organs such as liver, heart, and brain are produced, or whether necessary nutrients are used up. The control system is also what prevents an eye from growing from a fingertip. Without such a control, this could happen because the genes that code for eye structure are also present in the hand. In fact, every single cell contains the full set of blueprints for the whole life form it represents. It is difficult to imagine — but nonetheless quite true — that a tiny cell in your fingertip is packed with all the DNA information required to construct another you, as identical as a photocopy is to the original typescript.

The genes are all there. But each cell expresses itself in a different way, that is, it uses its information differently. Cells, then, are not different because they contain different information — it is simply a matter of how they use the identical information they have. It is well to remember that if the on-off mechanism malfunctions, birth defects and cancer may show up, and so, too, may the changes we call aging.

Let's go back to our original question — what is it that causes normal cells to run out of power so that they do not continue to divide forever? Unfortunately, we don't know exactly. Unicellular organisms — algae, yeasts, bacteria and amoebas — appear to have no programmed life span. They seem to be able to divide and redivide, on and on, until they are killed off by structural changes or something hostile in their environment. Why can't we do the same? One answer is that it's probably because we reproduce sexually by mingling genetic material, and those other life forms do not enjoy that pleasurable

method of propagation. They merely subdivide asex-
ually. It has much to do with evolution and the speculation that mortality became necessary for higher organisms like men and women for the simple reason that they
needed room to grow, to adapt and develop. Immortality
would mean overcrowding, slower reproduction and
evolution. It is almost as though to adapt and survive
and be endowed with intellect, we must be programmed
to fail and die. It is another of the ironies that dot the
story of aging. If this is the case, there might well be
something in our cells — perhaps a "death gene" or an
"aging gene" — passed along from some dim time when
DNA first arranged itself into the complex order that
spelled out human life. This hypothetical gene, coded
for age, shuts us all down when the time comes.

Hayflick says that our genetic program is wound like
an alarm clock at conception, and it plays out its message over eighty to one hundred years. When the program is all over, that's it. "From an evolutionary standpoint," he believes, "nature selects for survival only long
enough to propagate itself, just as rocket engineers don't
worry about which system will fail in a space probe after
it completes a Mars flyby." All of the genetic information
exchange that takes place when egg and sperm meet —
or when a DNA-loaded cancer virus invades a normal
cell — resets or reprograms the biological clock. As Hayflick puts it: "The genetic cards are reshuffled." Survival
of the species is guaranteed by this mechanism, but we
as individuals are doomed to fail — by program.

The key word in all of it, when everything is said and

done, is information. Without the right information, problems arise. A single error in the genetic code — a "word" misspelled or a "paragraph" misplaced — can induce a complicated disease involving many organs. Important chemicals may not be made if the production line breaks down or malfunctions, or they could accumulate in dangerous amounts, clogging the body's brain and arteries. A coding mistake in DNA can lead to the wrong kind of protein being made.

Scientists have been suggesting for some time that errors in the genetic code could have something to do with the aging process. Genetic material might become faulty with age, and it loses its memory, as it were. The result is flawed protein and bodily slowdown. Several researchers lean to the idea that DNA degeneration may be due to errors piled up during the repetitive copying process. All of the unraveling and raveling that DNA undergoes during subdivision and protein synthesis increases the risk of damage to the copying mechanism, until finally the cell's damage control machinery is unable to deal with the cumulative accidents. If DNA becomes an inaccurate blueprint, then trouble is sure to result.

Such errors may be accidental or, as some researchers believe, actually programmed into specific "aging genes" that are responsible for ensuring that a certain number of mistakes take place during the manufacture of protein. External forces such as radiation, both ultraviolet sunlight and medical x-rays, can trigger DNA errors. Viruses, drugs, and pollutants that penetrate to the cell's nucleus where they interfere with the business of genetic information handling and metabolism are also error-producers.

We observed earlier that hibernating animals live longer at lower temperatures. Recent experiments have shown that *high* temperatures interfere with chemical reactions within the cell, just as radiation and other outside agents do, causing a faster buildup of detrimental waste products that can shorten longevity. Rats maintained at lower temperatures, for example, survive almost three months longer than rats living at higher temperatures. It is also known that cultured hamster cells have a reproductive life span that is strongly dependent on temperature. In one recent experiment at the University of Kentucky, in fact, the death rate of hamster cells increased by a factor of 5,000 — from a value of 0.002 hours to a value of 10 hours — as temperature was increased from 37° C. to 46° C.

The association between DNA damage and aging was made dramatically visible recently by Dr. Robert L. Herrmann, a Boston University biochemist. While examining mouse liver and brain DNA strands under an electron microscope, he found a number of looped, hairpin-shaped branches in the genetic material of older animals. The loops, it was suggested, may imprison the genes, preventing them from participating in cell reproduction and protein synthesis. Whether excessively stable chemical bonds build up between the double strands as a result of the untwisting and retwisting or whether foreign protein has invaded the cell are questions that remain to be answered. "If the loops are indeed the culprit in old age," says Dr. Herrmann, "then it's not unrealistic to imagine we can find a safe drug to prevent or eliminate them."

One of the most important error theories of aging has been formulated by Dr. Leslie E. Orgel of the Salk Institute for Biological Studies in San Diego. His idea is that during the routine synthesis of protein, the wrong amino acid will every so often be inserted into the protein chain under construction. When such an event occurs, according to the theory, there is an increasing accumulation of errors in protein that eventually leads to an "error catastrophe" and the synthesis of faultier and faultier proteins. The end result is that the cell machinery grinds to a stop. An analogy that illustrates Orgel's theory is of a factory that produces equipment used by a second factory. If the first factory makes a defective piece of equipment, the second factory will turn out poor products. If in turn the product of the second factory is machinery utilized by a third, that second piece of equipment will be poorer than the first, with the third factory's product sure to be worse than all the others. Orgel has argued that the aging of clones (descendants) of cells such as those studied by Hayflick could be due to a catastrophic breakdown in the accuracy of protein synthesis in the cytoplasm which, as noted earlier, lies outside the cell nucleus. Since the machinery responsible for synthesizing proteins is itself made up of proteins, if that apparatus becomes inadequate, it goes on to produce even less adequate protein-making machinery in the next generation.

Experiments with fruit flies, which progress from fertilized egg to old age in a matter of days and are, thus, an ideal model for aging studies, have tended to support Orgel's theory. In one such experiment, British scientists nurtured fruit-fly larvae on amino acids that interfere with the functions of protein. They did this in an effort to create repeating errors in the continuous protein-making process. The adult flies, it turned out, had much shorter life spans than flies from larvae raised on the right base acids.

If Orgel is correct — and also Denham Harman who suggests that damaging free radicals are produced outside the nucleus in the mitochondria — the implications for longevity research could be quite important. The cytoplasm and its mitochondria are, of course, more accessible than the nucleus for antiaging chemotherapy such as vitamin E. Recall also that the ribosomes, workshops where proteins are assembled, are also out in the cytoplasm. These, too, would be more accessible to drugs that could extend the production of protein beyond the time age slows it down. This, in fact, has been done in test tubes, using drugs such as cortisone which may boost production of ribosomes and RNA. The increases, however, have been moderate.

Easier access to non-nuclear parts of the cell is also important to any future experiments involving the transplantation of hardier genetic material from a young person to an older one. Or, the splicing in of synthesized "young" genetic material. One way to edit out the wrong genes — which is what such grafting is all about — is through controversial experiments with recombinant DNA, the joining together of DNA from different organisms. Scientists now know that DNA is present not only in the nuclei of cells but in other parts of the cell as well. For instance, DNA has been detected in chloroplasts in green plants. These power plants, located outside the nucleus, do the job of photosynthesis, the process by which plants convert light energy from the sun directly into chemical energy. DNA also exists in the mitochondria and in tiny circular particles called plasmids that float free in the cells of bacteria. Since these DNA types are not confined within the walls of the nucleus or caught up in the hum of its complex machinery, scientists can, as we have said, get at them easier. And they have done this. By fusing bits of DNA from different sources and inserting them into bacteria where they can grow as the bacteria divide and redivide, scientists can create something new. Besides endowing plants with new synthetic capabilities, recombinant DNA research, with its bacteria factories, could be used to produce vast quantities of a new protein or chemical that would do new things, or simply to produce large quantities of others that are either in short supply or not easily obtainable with current methods. Or, one might grow new animals with characteristics they could never acquire in nature — not exactly a cow that would produce chocolate milk by combining its genes with those from cacao plants, but possibly one that might be endowed with the much longer life span of an Indian elephant, thus enabling it to produce more milk for many more years. There may not, of course, be a specific gene that codes for aging, but other beneficial hereditary traits might be fused into an animal that lacked them, thus adding to its other assets. It is tempting, and admittedly more facetious than scientific, to speculate on what might happen if gerontologists could splice genes from a California bristlecone pine into those of humans, giving us all great-grandfather clocks of aging.

Which is as good a way as any to bring us back to Leonard Hayflick and his cellular clock of aging. He, too, has tested Orgel's theory of accumulated errors, by comparing the production of virus in young and old cultured cells to determine if errors in protein manufacture show up faster in the older. The rationale behind his experiment is the virus's ability to replicate by utilizing the host's cells' synthesizing mechanism. If defective material does accumulate in old cells, as theorized by Orgel, then virus which replicates in old cells would show evidence of faulty maturation. (Viruses, once inside a cell, take over its machinery, including the instructions for normal duplication. Tricked by the virus's frantic commands, and with its own genetic information altered or blotted out, the hapless cell is forced to manufacture thousands of new viruses instead of normal protein before destroying itself, or it may be so transformed that it produces copies of its new, flawed self, the end result of which could be a cancer.) In Hayflick's experiment, no differences in replication were noted between the young and old cells, implying that the synthesizing machinery used by the viruses continued to function accurately with age.

Hayflick has been trying to determine whether the genetic clock is in the nucleus or the cytoplasm. He has been doing this by transplanting nuclei from, say, old cells to the cytoplasm of younger ones to find out if such a fusion will affect doubling. If, for instance, the older cell continues to replicate beyond the Hayflick limit after it has combined with young cytoplasm, this would indicate that doubling regulation lies outside the nucleus. Preliminary results have convinced him that the clock does reside in the nucleus. "If further studies confirm this, it would render less tenable those theories of aging like the 'error theory' that depend on misspecified proteins being produced in the cytoplasm," he says.

Althought a number of researchers feel it is premature to accept the notion that obsolescence is programmed into our cells — citing cases where cell lines in culture have been kept alive longer with drugs and vitamins — Hayflick sticks to his theory. And his work has had a monumental impact on other research. His is also a most logical theory, when one considers that humankind and everything else that lives dies after so many days, months or years. Also, as Hayflick points out, if all the multitude of animal cell types were continually renewed — without loss of function or capacity for self-renewal — one would expect that the organs composed of such cells would function normally indefinitely, and that their host would live on forever. "Unhappily, however," he says, "renewal cell populations do not occur in most tissues, and when they do, a proliferative finitude is often manifest."

There was considerable skepticism, if not outright rejection, when Hayflick's theory first appeared in the journals. The scientist, in fact, has a letter from one of the most prestigious, telling him, "The largest fact to have come out from tissue culture in the last fifty years is that cells inherently capable of multiplying will do so indefinitely if supplied with the right milieu in vitro [in the test tube]." Of that rejection, Hayflick has remarked: "I cite this incident not to be unkind but to illustrate the continuing necessity for retention of an open mind in science. Dogmas did not die in the last century. They are still present. Many of today's most cherished beliefs will surely fall before some young iconoclast tomorrow. Regrettably, heretical views are still as untolerated in science as they are in theology. Nevertheless, many of today's scientific truths are rooted in yesterday's heresy. Having had first-hand experience with the promotion of a heresy, I can tell you that old dogmas do not die an easy death. Even today, some years after our initial report of the finite lifetime of cultured normal human fibroblasts, and its confirmation in literally hundreds of laboratories throughout the world, there remain several persons who are unwilling to accept the fact, to say nothing of the interpretation.

"In England, there is an active group who also hold a minority view even after the accumulation of five hundred years' worth of scientific data. They are members of the Flat Earth Society who hold steadfastly that the earth is not a sphere at all. Nevertheless, their right to hold a minority view I would support in the manner of Voltaire."

To the casual observer, Hayflick points out, the notion that cultured, normal human embryo fibroblasts will die after several months of vigorous division extending over fifty population doublings is a difficult one to accept.

Yet, he adds, the same logic that accepts aging and death in whole animals as being universal and inevitable often results in disbelief when the same phenomenon is witnessed in cells cultured from those same animals. "Is it possible that the same psychological barrier that denies the inevitability of our own deaths influences the reluctance to accept the finitude in the proliferative capacity of our cultured cells?" he asks. "This may represent a new area for investigation by the psychologists and psychiatrists in this society which could provide an unique bridge between our respective disciplines."

A final note before we leave Leonard Hayflick. There are two interesting diseases that mimic aging, and because they do, gerontologists believe they may help unravel the mysteries of genuine aging. The disorders are progeria and Werner's syndrome, and they are cited as further evidence for cellular clocks. Progeria is a rare disorder, a freak of nature that is a curious mixture of infantilism and premature senility afflicting the very young. Children with the disease retain their milk teeth and lack body hair, but they exhibit all the other physical characteristics of age — loose and wrinkled skin, receding chins, narrow chests, dwarfed, stooping posture. They are mentally and physically old, grotesquely so, long before their time. Most, in fact, succumb to heart disease before they reach maturity. Youngsters with the disorder also have lipofuscin accumulation in their cells. But more important, the cells of progerics do not divide more than ten times — almost as if they had quickly and prematurely lived out the forty or so doublings that an old cell would have experienced.

Werner's syndrome is a similar disorder, except that it is known to be an inherited one. (The evidence for genetic transmission of progeria is unclear.) Dr. Stephen Fulder of Chelsea College in London has studied the syndrome and found numerous similarities between its symptoms and those of normal old age. A gene or genes, he theorizes, speeds up the "aging" process by mutation. Moreover — and here is the heart of his experiments — while the cells of Werner's patients appear normal, they multiply and divide only a dozen times before they die — as opposed to the approximately fifty times a normal cell divides over a normal life span.

It really makes no difference whether these two diseases are representative of a genuine aging process. Of importance is that the changes occurring with them are noticeable on the cell level and in the outward physical appearance of the individuals suffering from them. Something is going on inside, something is amiss. Chances are a genetic clock of one kind or another is the timekeeper since the changes that arrive with each of these disorders are the very same ones that occur with normal aging. The only difference is that they show up long before their time. They could not, then, be due to ordinary wear and tear. Says Fulder: "There is in all likelihood a single defective gene product in Werner's syndrome that profoundly influences the aging rate. The discovery of its identity would be an important step towards the understanding of the primary causes of aging."

Does all of this mean, then, that because of preset

cellular clocks science is limited in its efforts to inhibit aging on a cellular level? Are extra years through a more favorable environment the only answer? At our current level of knowledge, the answer to both, unfortunately, is yes. I believe, however, that research in cellular aging represents science's ultimate challenge, and that one day gerontologists will find a way to suppress biological aging — a process that might be likened to playing a record turntable at a slower speed. We have already mentioned some of the ways this might be done — adding various substances to cell cultures, slowing up free radical production with antioxidants. Certainly the great strides that cell biologists have made recently in creating artificial genes, along with their work with recombinant DNA, would caution against a totally negative response to the question, Can we do it?

Hayflick does not tell us the quest is impossible. He tells us, rather, if I read him correctly, that there is this limit, and that if we are ever to achieve the dream of the alchemists we must do something about the basic process of aging at the cellular level. It doesn't matter how many degenerative diseases we wipe out or ward off. It is the clock itself that we must get at. Life span, he says, could increase if we could "reprogram the tape" through drug treatment or by using a synthetic DNA. This would enable cells to double more than the average fifty times, and thus live longer.

For the moment, though, possibly it is a good thing for us laypeople to think of Hayflick's limit as just that — a limit to what we can ever be. For then we will have to concentrate on the quality of life, on adding life to years rather than years to life. It may be time for us to set the clock on the shelf, and polish it up and keep it running for as long as possible, but at the same time stop listening to its tick, and bemoaning the passage of time and the wear and tear on this delicate instrument.

Part IV

Making
the Best of It

Chapter Eleven

GIVEN THE FACT that so many journalists are biased toward simplification and exaggeration, it is understand-
able that one of the media's favorite "enterprise" stories
is the one based on an interview with an octogenarian or
older, the purpose being to ferret out that elderly individual's recipe for long life. Hayflick's limit plays no part
in such articles — indeed, most newspaper editors have
never heard of the man or his work — and this is probably a good thing if you're an editor who is aware that a
newspaper's job is to entertain as well as to inform, and
knows also the old tabloid dictum about never cluttering
a good story with the facts.

In the years when my background in science was on
the light side, I wrote a lot of "long life recipe" stories,
and the replies to my stock questions were contradictory
and trite. I take some heart in the possibility, however,
that the old-timers with whom I talked and read about
in my newspaper's clip library were really putting us all

on — that they knew they were expected to say something bright for the readers. I wish, now, that just one of them would have told me the truth when I posed the question about the recipe, saying something like, "Because I'm a lucky old son-of-a-bitch, that's how I got this far." But they never did. And so we read, hear, and cheer about the likes of Joshua Seitlein of Brooklyn who celebrated his hundredth birthday, fueled each and every day by three pints of hard liquor, six glasses of beer and a strong Russian pipe, along with much strong tea and a staple diet of potatoes, fat and herring swimming in sweet oil. We probably boo and hiss, human nature being what it is, the likes of poor Orvel S. Dorman of Rome, New York, who passed his hundredth birthday hale and hearty, saying he never ever used tobacco, was a Prohibitionist, and never used foul language, either. His long life, he said when pressed by a reporter who must have wondered how he was going to get the story in the paper, had much to do with a "clear conscience, plenty of hard work, absence of worry and minding my own business."

In the light of such conflicting prescriptions for longevity, it would be quite permissible to throw up one's hands in frustration and fall back on the precise mechanisms of genetic inheritance which, in effect, tell us that the only way to live long is to choose one's parents. We cannot, of course, do any such thing, and neither can the genetic engineers, despite the startling progress they have made in the manipulation of DNA.

The genetic laws of nature, however — important though they may be in governing our life spans — need not necessarily be roadblocks. For, although total life span in every species is genetically determined, our own life-styles and the events that go on about us can and do affect that basic genetic program. We are speaking, of course, of a multitude of environmental factors, those hard-to-ignore influences that are so hopelessly intertwined with the genetic. These factors — among them diet, occupation, exercise, economic status, geography and mental attitude — are most important to the aging process and, according to many gerontologists, are responsible for wide variations in life expectancy among human beings. A recent United Nations report referred to these factors as "collective toxicomanias," and included in the list tobacco, alcohol, tranquilizers, even television.

Dr. Stephen P. Jewett, the late professor emeritus of psychiatry at New York Medical College, is among those who point out that even though heredity is the most conspicuous of the factors that combine to determine our life spans, the actual span and the potential one may be quite different. Thus, a person who has inherited a lengthy potential life span may be outlived by someone who has not. He chose a bullet to illustrate this. Assume, Jewett says, that one has a bullet of a given size, shape and weight encased in a cartridge with a given amount of a certain type of explosive behind it. Such a cartridge, when exploded, will carry the bullet, under ideal conditions, a very long and definite distance before it gradually reaches the ground. A second bullet, all the factors being identical, would carry the bullet the same distance. Quite obviously, says Jewett, there are conditions in the pathway of the bullet that might impede its momentum and bring it to earth sooner. "The bullet is the individual, and the explosive is the genetic factor of his longevity potential. The factors encountered by the individual are the many which impair his vitality and prevent his reaching his potential life span. They may be so catastrophic as to stop him dead."

But, Jewett finds a flaw in his analogy. For while the bullets could be considered identical, such a comparison could only be assumed in humans because in actual life, no two are ever exactly alike. "The bullet carries within it no self-destructive forces, whereas the human being may carry many, either genetically or environmentally induced. These forces are frequently as disastrous as any he might encounter in his external environment which prevent his reaching his potential life span. We have only to cite the large number of accident-prone individuals and the suicides which take such a toll."

It would appear, according to Jewett, that certain individuals also have — either genetically laid down or acquired through having been exposed from their inception to the right dynamic and physical environment — another set of forces. These contain none of those self-destructive ones and permit our life spans to achieve their potential. "This has enabled some to deal with many stress situations, as well as to avoid many, and to maintain a continued pattern of homeostasis so necessary for health and a long life span."

Several questions are raised by all of this. One is whether an individual can, by giving thought, add even a week to his or her potential life span. The answer appears to be an unequivocal no. Neither the individual nor science, at the moment, has any absolute control over the genes of heredity. But there is, on the other hand, another question, a somewhat different one. Can one, by giving thought, help a life span reach its potential? Or, for that matter, by not giving thought, prevent it? The answer here is yes, to a certain degree. And what it all boils down to is controlling the controllable factors in our environment and developing a sensible life-style. This approach, of course, means trying to postpone the onset of certain physical and emotional illnesses by such means as proper nutrition, proper use of mental capacities, and balanced amounts of exercise and relaxation. It means forgetting, for a while, the genes, important though those bits of DNA are.

As we said earlier, many gerontologists feel that environmental factors are responsible for the sometimes sharp variations in the life expectancy statistics of countries and localities, with the differences often reflecting the degree of a region's mental, physical and social health. For example, Upper Volta and Gabon, in West Africa, have the shortest life expectancy — 31 years for females, 25 years for males. Contrast those figures with Sweden, which ranks at the top, having a life expectancy of 76.54 years for female infants, 71.85 for males. Norway is next with 76.83 for females, 71.09 for males. In the United States, life expectancy for female whites is around 76.4 years, 68.5 for males. For nonwhite female babies in the U.S., it is 68.9 years, 60.5 for males. The edge that women have over men is an important one to consider in any discussion of the influence of environment on longevity. As of now, in the United States there are sixty-nine men for every one hundred women sixty-five and older — compared to forty years ago when the ratio was nearly even. By the year 2000, according to the Census Bureau, there will be about sixty-five males for every one hundred females in the over-sixty-five category. Whether the gap will ever narrow is debatable. Some demographers point to subtle indications that among European women, at least, the life expectancy seems to be decreasing. They attribute this to heavier alcohol and cigarette consumption, and the increased entry of women into the labor market. Heart attacks could become more frequent and deadlier in women than they are at present, a situation that could easily develop as women find themselves confronted with the combined strain of housekeeping, motherhood and employment, particularly if the job involves a serious career.

Infant mortality rates, also, are lower among those in a higher socioeconomic bracket, and there is substantial evidence — although the issue remains controversial — that the racial differentiation that gives whites a more favorable longevity pattern is due to economic and social factors. Inadequate health care, the high incidence of violent crime, emotional strain and poor dietary habits — all of these ingredients that go with living on the bottom line affect longevity. That bleak picture, however, may be showing some signs of changing for the better. Just before the turn of the century, American blacks had a life expectancy somewhere around fifteen years less than whites. Since then, the gap has narrowed considerably, due, in all probability, to socioeconomic improvement and increasing efforts to get better medicine into the ghetto. Now only a few percentage points separate the races. Black males, too, it has been found, suddenly seem to last longer and in better shape than whites if they make it to seventy-five or so. "Perhaps," speculates Dr. Robert N. Butler, director of the National Institute on Aging, "it's a survival of the fittest. If they can make it that long, then they are made of such tough stuff that it's likely they will live some years longer."

With that as background, let's take a closer look at some of the environmental factors that influence human longevity, particularly those we can do something about. It would be well to remember, however, that much of the payoff in extra years that is associated with these factors results from the avoidance of disease, rather than from any actual halting of the aging process. Also, even though we must discuss these factors separately, they often interact and rarely operate independently, no more than nature and nurture do when shaping any given individual.

DIET

Nothing is more important for the body's well-being than the food and drink it is given. What we eat and how much are key factors in weight maintenance and in long life.

The kind of food we eat is obviously important, for we all need a proper balance of carbohydrates, saturated and unsaturated fats, proteins, vitamins and minerals.

Food fads and crash diets — "organic" foods, Zen macro-
biotics, high protein, grapefuit and eggs, and near starvation levels of bouillon and spicy tomato juice — are
generally on shaky biochemical ground and have made
more money for their touts than sense for the followers.
Any benefits derived from such lackluster regimens slip
quickly backward once the faddists tire, as they will, of
the lack of variety. There is also a good possibility that
these diets do a great deal of damage to health over the
long haul — and to longevity — because of the lack of
necessary nutrients.

Among the more responsible scientists who have
turned their attention to diet and its effect on longevity
was Elie Metchnikoff (Chapter Seven) whose theories,
some of which do not withstand the test of current scientific inquiry, nevertheless bear mentioning because of
recent related research. Referring to a mechanism he
called intestinal putrefaction, Metchnikoff observed that
bacterial decomposition as food passed through the large
bowel was what shortened the life span of every living
creature. "It is indubitable," he remarked, "that the intestinal microbes or their poisons may reach the system
generally and bring harm to it. I infer from the facts that
the more a digestive tract is charged with microbes, the
more it is a source of harm capable of shortening life. As
the large intestine not only is the part of the digestive
tube most richly charged with microbes, but is relatively
more capacious in mammals than in any other verte-
brates, it is a just inference that the duration of life of
mammals has been notably shortened as the result of
chronic poisoning from an abundant intestinal flora." To

prove his contention that the longer the colon the shorter the life span, Metchnikoff surveyed a variety of life, from long-lived birds with no large bowel to short-lived mammals with long ones. He noted that ruminants — animals such as cows, sheep and giraffes that graze and chew the cud stored in the first of the stomach's four chambers — have a good deal of intestinal putrefaction and short lives. On the other hand, birds such as parrots — which have no large intestine in which to accumulate excreta and intestinal bacteria — enjoy much longer lives. Metchnikoff did confess to being baffled by one animal that did not follow his colon-longevity rule: the elephant. This mammal, possessed of an enormous large intestine and a capacious cecum (the beginning of the large bowel) is capable of living for a century. Complained the Russian: "I have had no opportunity of investigating the elephant from this point of view, and have no explanation to suggest."

Metchnikoff also focused on dietary elements themselves, primarily during an anthropological trip among the Kalmucks in the steppes of western Russia. Carrying out comparative physical measurements of the inhabitants, he noticed that their physical development was slower than that of Caucasians. The arrested growth with its postponement of the usual outward signs of aging, he later concluded, was due to their habit of drinking fermented milk. Certain that yogurt and other cultured milk products were teeming with the right bacteria to rid the intestinal system of the poisonous bacilli that caused putrefaction, Metchnikoff began eating sour milk products regularly. He even ate quantities of the bacteria neat. "For more than eight years," he reported, "I took as a regular part of my diet, soured milk, at first prepared from boiled milk, inoculated with a lactic leaven. . . . I am very well pleased with the results, and I think my experiment has gone on long enough to justify my view. Several of my friends, some of whom suffered from maladies of the intestine or kidneys, have followed my example, and have been well satisfied. I think, therefore, that lactic bacteria can render a great service in the fight against intestinal putrefaction." If it was true, according to Metchnikoff, that precocious and unhappy old age was due to poisoning of the tissues, with the bulk of the poison coming from the large intestine with its swarms of microbes, then it was clear that agents which arrest intestinal putrefaction must at the same time postpone and ameliorate old age. This theoretical view, he felt, was confirmed by data on races that live chiefly on soured milk and whose members have great age in common.

Inevitably, Metchnikoff's name was linked to a commercial yogurt product — the manufacturer advertised that he was the "sole provider to Professor Metchnikoff" — but the scientist received no profit from the association. Journalists, being the skeptics they are, insinuated that the opposite was true, that Metchnikoff had made a fortune from the deal. He survived the criticism, however, and hung on to the respect of his fellow scientists, who, although they found his intestinal approach to longevity a bit difficult to follow, could not ignore his position in the Pasteur Institute nor his stature as a researcher.

While yogurt may not be an elixir of youth, it is known to have a beneficial effect in various bowel and skin conditions, particularly among the aged, and it is low in calories, which is probably the chief reason that some 100,000 tons of the fermented stuff are eaten each year in the United States alone.

Yogurt's effects in the intestines and Metchnikoff's ideas about bowel putrefaction are no more offbeat, in the final analysis, than some of the current thinking about such things as roughage in the diet. Roughage is a category of bulky, indigestible foods such as bran that acts as an intestinal irritant. Popularized as the save-your-life diet by Dr. David Reuben, who also gave us everything we wanted to know about sex, roughage is supposed to ward off a number of diseases, cancer among them. This theory, which has been seized on by the cereal manufacturers, who of course "make no medical claims," is based on the suspected link between the widespread use of refined carbohydrates, such as white flour and sugar, and cancer of the large bowel. The suggestion is that these refined staples of the American diet pass more slowly through the gut than roughage and unrefined foods, and this may increase the colon's exposure to cancer-causing agents. There is, in fact, statistical data to support this.

It has been shown that American blacks appear to be developing malignancies of the colon and rectum at rates that are nearing those of whites — while native Africans still have a low frequency, due possibly to their dietary habits, which include large amounts of roughage and unabsorbable cellulose (plant fiber). These have a faster transit time through the intestines. Stomach cancer, too, appears to be more prevalent among populations whose diet consists mainly of starchy foods such as potatoes, rice and bread, and which does not emphasize cereals, fresh fruits and vegetables.

One ought to be aware, however, that some commercially sold bran cereals, which are popular among high-fiber dieters, contain large amounts of sugar — and excess sugar can be a problem, not only for diabetics, but particularly for those who have heart disease and high levels of an important form of body fat, triglycerides. The average American, it has been estimated, eats around two to three pounds of the sweet carbohydrate every week. Scientists are concerned about such intake because a carbohydrate can be converted into fats, and these can clog arteries. If a person has a history of artery-clogging disease, the conversion process of extra carbohydrate calories to fat is aggravated. Even without such a medical history there may be a danger. One British study, for example, suggests that those who consume more than a quarter of a pound of sugar a day are five times more apt to suffer heart attacks than those who eat smaller amounts. The role of sugar as a causative factor in hypertension is also under investigation.

So much for the sorts of things we take into our systems. Equally as important is how much we eat. As the body slows down with age, it simply doesn't need as many calories as it did when it was younger. Too many calories can, of course, mean becoming overweight, and obesity in humans is known to reduce life span. On the other hand, there is strong evidence that restricting calorie intake dramatically increases the life span of rats, mice, flies, chickens, and that interesting aquatic creature, the rotifer. Along this line, the classic experiments were conducted in very young rats by Cornell's Clive McCay in the 1930s. McCay fed his animals diets sufficient in all nutrients but sharply reduced in calories, and not only retarded their growth until the calories were increased but extended their life spans by as much as forty percent. In one of his experiments, underfeeding the rats enabled them to live up to 1,450 days, while feeding a normal diet gave them no more than 965 days. Furthermore, with the extended life span of the rats, there was also a delay in the onset of chronic diseases related to senescence and tumors.

McCay's work has been repeated many times and extended to include other species, such as the rotifer. Experiments with these tiny animals have succeeded in prolonging their life spans to forty-five and fifty-five days (the normal life span, as we mentioned in our discussion of temperature lowering techniques, is thirty-four days) by reducing their food intake and by lowering the temperature of the water in which they live.

No one knows why McCay's experiments worked the way they did, but it has been suggested that the mechanism may be immunological. We have seen that as we age, we become more susceptible to disease, and that this is a result of our declining immune system. The elderly do not fight infection as easily as the young do, and their weakened immune systems find it more difficult to tell the difference between their own normal cells and all the harmful, outside agents, including cancer cells. Recently,

UCLA's Dr. Roy C. Walford put mice on low calorie diets, and not only doubled their life spans but apparently stopped them from developing as many cancers as mice fed normal diets. The suggestion here is that by slowing the aging process through caloric restriction, the immune system stays tuned and disease is fought off as it would be in a younger animal. Walford's mice did, in fact, undergo marked changes in immune response as a result of dietary restriction, retaining good immune function beyond the time that it was on the decline in other mice. The age-related development of autoimmunity — in which the body fails to recognize its own cells and attacks and damages them — also was apparently suppressed.

Whether or not the human life span can be lengthened significantly by cutting calories has not yet been scientifically proven. Scientists who are wary of extrapolating the results of dietary restriction studies from animals to people without adequate clinical trials explain that the majority of the lab work involves underfeeding very young animals. Such a regimen noticeably stunts their growth, and feeding comparable low-calorie diets to children would undoubtedly make them subnormal in height and also more prone to disease. This, of course, is one of the classic dilemmas confronting researchers who often must balance risk against benefit. In the case of drugs, sooner or later every one that has been tested in animals and used eventually in humans has to be administered to some person for the first time. The researchers' reasoning is that since it had not proved damaging in extensive animal testing it probably will not prove harmful to humans and might, indeed, do some good. Such clinical testing, though, would be morally unacceptable if the patient were not fully informed about the risk-benefit ratio or, to add another variable, if there were no animal model for the disease the researcher is attempting to cure. Deliberately withholding nourishing protein from an infant would be condemned by the vast majority of researchers. The scientists, therefore, must rely on field observations of undernourished humans who live in underdeveloped countries, or people who, as part of their culture, follow rather unusual dietary habits.

One who has studied the effects of the serious problem of malnutrition in this way is Dr. Joaquim Cravioto, a Mexico City pediatrician who has accumulated a wealth of experience caring for children suffering from a protein-deficiency disease called kwashiorkor. First discovered in 1933, the disorder is endemic to a number of tropical and subtropical countries. It occurs primarily in infants who have been weaned onto starchy foods, such as manioc root in Africa, that contain very little protein. The child gets plenty of calories and appears well-nourished, to the point of developing a characteristic "pot belly" and generalized swelling of body tissues. The child actually is suffering from serious malnutrition because of the protein deficiency and its accompanying lack of essential amino acids. In their studies with kwashiorkor patients in Mexico and Guatemala, Dr. Cravioto and his associates showed that the short stature for their age, due to malnutrition, was accompanied by poorer performance on psychological tests. As kwashiorkor patients became better nourished, their behavioral skills improved somewhat, but there was an interesting exception. Infants who underwent nutritional rehabilitation before they were six months old continued to be deficient in their test behavior, suggesting that acute malnourishment during those first six months could be permanently damaging to IQ and behavior. While such observations have not found a link between diet and longevity, they are, nonetheless, valuable for what they tell us of the importance of protein in our diets.

Despite the lack of solid evidence that dietary restrictions improve the human life span, the concept still makes a good deal of sense if only for the simple reason that excessive calories make one overweight — and obesity is a major life-shortening factor. More calories than we need increases our risk of heart, kidney and blood vessel diseases that cut short our years. It is also known that our requirements for all sorts of food decrease with age. This applies not only to our requirements and tolerance for starches and sugars, but for fats, amino acids and proteins. According to Dr. Nathaniel O. Calloway of the University of Wisconsin, during the years of rapid growth we need these substances in order to build body tissues. As time goes on we pass the point of maximum development — somewhere around eighteen for the female and twenty-five for the male — the need for proteins and amino acids that build them has diminished to a point where they should be reduced in the diet. This is because aging adults slowly lose muscle mass. If food is not reduced, the muscles are replaced by fat. Even an individual who maintains his or her weight throughout adult life is, in fact, gaining in fat and losing protein.

There is no satisfactory evidence, says Calloway, that increasing amino acids or protein intake in the diet in any way lengthens life or forestalls the aging process. In fact, he says, there is evidence to show that high protein intake throughout life may hasten death from senescence. Calloway believes that the most desirable state from the standpoint of energy intake including fats, carbohydrates and protein is to be underweight since such a person statistically survives longer than the overweight one. There is also no evidence, says Calloway, that requirements for vitamins increase with age; after maturity, also, the individual needs only small amounts of replacement calcium, iron, sodium, potassium and magnesium. (Insofar as vitamins are concerned, some, such as A and D, are known to be needed in smaller quantities.)

In the entire discussion of the benefits to longevity of low caloric intake, however, there is no more dramatic evidence in its favor than that uncovered in recent studies of unique, long-living groups of individuals. Reputedly blessed with many members well over 100 years old, these superaged people live in mountainous regions of the world — in places like Vilcabamba, in the Andes of Ecuador; Hunza, near Tibet; and Abkhasia, in the Soviet Republic of Georgia. Although there are some doubts about their supercentenarian status — valid documentation of their age, for instance, is not generally available — there is little question that they do live to a remarkably old age. Among the most sought after members of this group — sought after both by scientists eager to study his circulation and journalists after his recipe for long life — was Shirali Muslimov, who before

he died at the reported age of 168 in 1973, was alleged
to be the oldest living human. Muslimov apparently
worked until his death as a watchman on a farm, riding
his donkey over five miles of mountain slopes to work
every day. He fathered his last child at the age of 130
and, according to his doctors, had a blood pressure typical of a man in his thirties. He had various explanations
for his longevity, depending on who asked. He told one
interviewer that it was "Allah and the Soviet power,"
another that it was "Lots of children and a good nature,"
and another that the secret was pure air and water, no
alcohol and no smoking.

How many extra-long-living people there are in the
Soviet Union is not known precisely. Vladimir Kyucharyants of the Novosti Press Agency made a trip through
the Caucasus during which he said he met and talked
with at least twenty elderly people ranging in age from
99 to 138. According to Kyucharyants, there are nearly
19,000 people nearly or over the age of 100 in the USSR.
(Social Security records indicate there are some 6,200
people 100 or older in a given year in the U.S.)

Just why these latter-day Methuselahs seem to live as
long as they do is a question that intrigues the droves of
Soviet and Western scientists who visit their isolated villages. Current speculation focuses on the two factors
these people have in common — a hilly environment and
rarefied atmosphere that require an incredible amount of
physical exertion merely to attend to daily living, and a
low calorie intake throughout life. Their diets, according to observers like Kyucharyants, generally contain 1,700
to 1,900 calories a day, compared to an average of 2,000

to 2,200 in the Soviet Union, and are relatively low in animal fats and carbohydrates. The average American, on the other hand, consumes excessive quantities of fat in a diet that totals 3,300 calories daily. Kyucharyants found that the diets of the hill people were typically high in vitamins due to the year-round consumption of fresh vegetables and fruit. "A Caucasian dinner is unheard of without tomatoes, cucumbers, all kinds of edible herbs, spring onions and garlic, which contain an abundance of phytoncides, substances that destroy pathogenic microbes in the organism," says the journalist, in a Metchnikovian aside. Apples, grapes, persimmons, and pomegranates are among the staple items, and pomegranate juice, rich in vitamin C, is used as a seasoning. Walnuts, with seventy percent fat content, are widely used. Rich in linoleic acid (an unsaturated fatty acid essential in nutrition), nut oil is credited with removing cholesterol and thus acts as an antisclerotic. Meat, including beef, goat and fowl, is eaten once or twice a week, according to Kyucharyants, and is mostly broiled. Bouillon soups and broths are avoided, and honey, high in food value, is used in place of processed sugar. Coffee and tea are not drunk, but a dry red wine of low alcoholic content is taken at all three meals. Many of the people visited by the Soviet journalist drink two ounces of homemade vodka twice a day, before meals. "A European would find Caucasian food too spicy," Kyucharyants observes. "But the local inhabitants are accustomed to it and they never suffer from heartburn. Such dairy foods as buttermilk and matsoni (a kind of yogurt) are consumed in great quantities, particularly buttermilk. All the people with whom I talked said that when they were thirsty, they drink it instead of water since it satisfied their thirst better, and according to physicians destroyed patho-genic microbes in the intestine."

Among the physicians who have visited Abkhasia in an effort to identify the factors common to exceptional longevity is Dr. Alexander Leaf of Harvard and the Massachusetts General Hospital. In 1971, under the sponsorship of the National Geographic Society, Dr. Leaf, armed with a stethoscope, blood pressure appa-ratus, ophthalmoscope, tuning fork and percussion ham-mer, went to the Caucasus, to Vilcabamba, and to the province of Hunza. He found a number of common de-nominators at work, including diet, among the long-living inhabitants of the three regions. In Vilcabamba, an agricultural community, Leaf noticed that the people lived almost exclusively on a vegetarian diet, with a daily caloric intake, according to another physician, of around 1,200. The inhabitants of Hunza, in the Kara-koram Mountains, also grow vegetables, grains, fruits and nuts but, Leaf found, not quite enough to last through the severe winters. "Before the new greens come through in the spring," he reported, "the people have gone through a period of semi-starvation. Theirs is ac-tually a bare subsistence economy. Caloric intake, by American standards, is low. In a survey of fifty-five adult male Hunzakuts, a Pakistani nutritionist, Dr. S. Maqsood Ali, had found an average daily intake of 1,923 calories, 50 grams of protein, 35 grams of fat, and 354 grams of carbohydrate. Animal protein and fat made up less than one percent of total daily intake. Judging from the

Vilcabambans and the Hunzakuts, the American Heart Association's advice is correct: stay lean, avoid animal fat, keep caloric intake down."

In the Caucasus, Leaf found a different picture. The economy was mixed agriculture-dairy, and animal products were eaten almost daily, including cheese, milk and yogurt. The cheese, which might give nutritionists pause, is, however, low in fat content, and the total fat intake is only around 40 to 60 grams a day. (In the U.S., according to the Department of Agriculture, the average daily fat intake is 157 grams. Ideally, say some nutritionists, we ought to reduce our fat intake to around thirty percent of our daily calories — ten percent each of poly-unsaturates, monounsaturates and saturates.) "Thus, the dietary factors uniform to all three areas I visited," said Leaf, "would seem to concur with the current weight of medical opinion: for long life, maintain a moderate caloric intake that generally avoids obesity, and a diet low in animal and saturated fats."

Leaf did not, of course, rule out the significance of heredity among the people he visited. The Hunzakuts, for instance, have been genetically isolated for some time and Leaf has speculated that a small number of individuals lacking "bad" genes — those that increase the probability of acquiring a fatal illness — settled in the valley hundreds of years before and that their isolation may have prevented a tainting of the strain. The elderly in Hunza, in fact, appears to Leaf to be related to one another, as did those in Vilcabamba. But in the Caucasus, the possible role of genetics seemed to be less strong. There, Leaf found many people over 100 who were not only Georgian but Russian, Armenian, and Turkish, which suggested that no single isolated genetic factor was involved in longevity. He saw this as confirming his view that controllable environmental factors are of significance. "On the other hand, heredity cannot be dismissed. When I spoke with many of the old people in the Caucasus, they proudly stated that they had either parents or siblings who also lived to be very old. When one asked a young person, of whatever ethnic background, in Abkhazia how long he or she expected to live, generally the answer was, 'To a hundred.' In proposing a toast to the health of a guest, they may exaggerate and say, 'May you live to be 300.' But 100 years as the normal lifespan is firmly established in their minds. This was confirmed by Dr. Georgi Kaprashvili, who lives and practices in the town of Gulripshi. It is not known how much high expectancy actually contributes to lifespan, but we agreed its effect must be positive."

We mentioned that not everyone accepts the claims of these long-lived folk. One of the skeptics is Zhores A. Medvedev, the exiled Russian biologist now working in London. Medvedev has attacked the widespread belief that there are many supercentenarians in the Caucasus, charging among other things that none of those believed to be from one hundred and twenty to one hundred and sixty-five years of age has been able to produce valid birth records, that the sections of the Caucasus which observe a ten-month Moslem year have more centenarians than Christian sectors, and that physiological and biochemical studies of the centenarians have produced the "paradoxical" finding that their function and metabolism are on the same level as those of people between fifty-five and sixty. Centenarians with well-established ages in other countries, he says, show degeneration more in keeping with their ages. Medvedev also ascribes the reputed longevity in the Caucasus to local honor and publicity surrounding the residents, factors which induce competition among villages and districts. He also points out that the reverence accorded the elderly is a stimulus to exaggerate age. There is also the fact that Stalin was Georgian. "In the post-war period, when Stalin was about 70 and rumors of his poor health started to circulate, official propagandists and political lecturers usually referred to the Georgian high longevity phenomenon to convince people about the possibilities of long life for the Dear Wise Teacher." Medvedev adds one more explanation: deserters from the army during the first and second world wars and during the Civil War forged birth certificates or used their fathers', thus exaggerating their age. He cites the widely-publicized case of a man reputed to be one hundred and thirty until a group of Ukrainian villagers recognized him as a World War I deserter and revealed his true age as seventy-eight. With hundreds of thousands of deserters on the loose during the wars, Medvedev believes that centenarians will keep turning up in many areas. "None of these cases of superlongevity are scientifically valid," he says. "They cannot be regarded as a gerontological phenomenon that promises the secrets of longevity. The only advice to be gained from the research, or pseudoresearch made of this superlongevity is rather banal, on the order of 'work with pleasure,' 'eat more cottage cheese,' 'don't

worry too much,' or 'live in the mountains.' Such simplistic 'environmental,' 'nutritional' and 'climatic' approaches to a radical increase of the maximum biological
limit of the evolutionarily-determined human lifespan do
not merit the name of science."

Nonetheless, it is difficult to fault the important role
that diet, physical activity and a proper frame of mind
play in a healthy, longer life. Insofar as diet is concerned, I might conclude with some good advice from
one Luigi Cornaro, a Venetian nobleman and architect
who was about one hundred years old when he died in
1565. He tells us that by the time he was thirty-five he
had begun to feel the ill effects of an intemperate life of
eating and drinking. He consulted physicians, the best of
his day, and they had but one bit of counsel for him —
he was to eat nothing but what agreed with him, but in
small quantities. Cornaro followed the advice, subsisting
from then on, on a daily diet of no more than twelve
ounces of solid food and fourteen ounces of wine. He
was never ill again, he said, except after the one time he
briefly gave up the diet. Cornaro recovered by going
back on the diet, observing, "What we leave after making a heavy meal does us more good than what we eat.
Our kind mother nature, in order that old men live still to
a greater age, has contrived matters so that they should
be able to subsist on as little as I do. For large quantities
of food cannot be digested by old and feeble stomachs."

Four hundred years later, Cornaro's advice remains
valid. Many nutritionists today suggest a daily intake of
no more than six ounces of protein (four ounces maximum to a serving), sixteen ounces of skim milk or the

equivalent in dairy products, more fruits and vegetables, and unrefined grain products. And what of Cornaro's fourteen ounces of wine a day? There is no question about the benefits of the beverage of the vine. Alcohol, notably in the form of wine, is one of the oldest drugs known to medicine. Hippocrates, the most celebrated Greek physician of antiquity, knew it could be used to fight infection. Ivan Pavlov used it to stimulate appetite, and the Persian king Cyrus the Great hauled it along on the march to Babylon to avoid disease caused by impure water. The Jewish physician Maimonides, the "second Moses" who became rabbi of Cairo, knew wine's digestive properties, remarking, "It contains much good and light nourishment. It is rapidly digested and helps to digest other foods. It also removes the superfluities from the pores of the flesh and excretes urine and perspiration. The older a man is, the more beneficial the wine is for him." Today, wine, the oldest, safest natural tranquilizer, is served in many hospitals and nursing homes throughout the United States to brighten meals and the often drab existence in such institutions. Study after study has demonstrated that serving wine in such settings improves interpersonal behavior, enabling friendships to be formed where indifference and apathy had existed previously. Wine also provides minerals that aid in tissue repair and regeneration, its iron content can combat anemia, and it resembles gastric juice more than any other natural beverage. And because of its antibacterial action, many physicians prescribe it for intestinal colic, colitis, diarrhea and a number of infections of the gastrointestinal tract.

Cornaro's fourteen ounces a day might be a bit heavy for some, particularly if the cup is drained in a single gulp. But still, as the Italians say, "A glass of wine works more wonders than a churchful of saints." Implicit in that, also, is moderation. One of the more interesting sidelights to this entire discussion — and one of those uplifting ones that we all like to hear in the midst of the doomsaying — is that data from insurance companies and general population surveys suggest that while heavy drinkers live shorter lives, moderate drinkers live the longest, longer even than abstainers. The abstainers, it turns out, are also struck by more heart attacks. The reasons behind this are not clear, although some researchers suggest that alcohol may exert some protective, tranquilizing effect on the heart. Another suggestion is that the moderate drinker is a person who knows how to relax and enjoy life, pluses in anyone's makeup.

The advice of Cornaro and all the others, the sages as well as the nutritionists, seems to be well taken — eat a little less than one is accustomed to, feed sparingly and defy the physician, light supper makes a long life, diet cures more than the lancet, he that eats but one dish seldom needs the doctor.

EXERCISE

As everyone knows, we need exercise to strengthen our muscles and force blood to circulate in the body's tissues where the cells build defenses against disease. And although it takes many hours of work to shed a single pound, exercise keeps artery-clogging cholesterol from building up too thickly and it helps establish new back-up systems of branch vessels — collateral circulation — that bring blood to the heart muscle. The more avenues blood has to the heart, the less chance there is for heart muscle to deteriorate and die in the event of an artery block. The nourishing blood simply flows past and around the blockage. Exercise also increases endurance, burns up a diabetic's excess sugar, reduces the ache of an ailing back, and relieves emotional tension by diverting to the muscles, where it does the most good, the anxious energy that results from stress.

Even a diet that is top-heavy with animal fats and protein may be offset by vigorous exercise performed regularly, although good sense should tell us that one cannot indulge routinely in enormous meals, drink heavily, and then expect that through some metabolic magic, exercise will cancel out the overindulgence.

Still, as one recent medical report put it, "To stay hearty, get sweaty." A classic study involving a group of Boston men and their Irish brothers points this up dramatically. The men in Ireland consumed huge quantities of eggs, butter, cream, bacon and other high-fat meats, but had a relatively low rate of coronary disease and hypertension. Their brothers in Boston, on the other hand, had a very high incidence of these disorders. Investigators found one variable that seemed to tell the story — exercise. The brothers in Ireland walked or bicycled several miles to work every day, work that involved heavy farming.

Another study involved former outstanding Finnish

long-distance runners and cross-country skiers, men ranging in age from forty to seventy-nine. Researchers found that the men had "younger" cardiopulmonary systems than a comparable group from a shopkeepers' association. A related study of 388 former athletes found a median life expectancy of seventy-two years — six to eight years longer than that of the general population above age fifteen. Still another study, this one involving British postal workers, found that deliverymen had fewer heart attacks and fewer fatal attacks than did clerks.

The most recent confirmation of exercise's value came during the 1978 scientific meeting of the American Heart Association. According to Stanford's Dr. Ralph S. Paffenbarger, Jr., who studied some 17,000 Harvard alumni, fatal and nonfatal heart attacks were lowest among the men who engaged in strenuous exercise on a regular basis — with the rate of heart attack twice as high in the sedentary grads. The study also showed that moderate exercise is better for the heart than very little and that subjects who were not athletic as students lessened their chances of suffering a heart attack by engaging in vigorous physical activity after graduation.

On his tour of the superage enclaves, Dr. Leaf found the level of physical activity and fitness to be striking among the elderly. Since regular exercise improves circulation in the body, including blood flow to the heart, gerontologists have concluded that the continuous physical activity of the residents of the three areas develops a good enough secondary supply to ensure circulation even in the event of artery-blocking atherosclerosis. "Given the choice," says Leaf, "most people will exert themselves as minimally as is compatible with daily existence. The people of Vilcabamba, Hunza and the Caucasus have no choice. They must keep physically active to survive."

It would be preposterous to claim that exercise is a sure way to roll back the years. Nothing, as we have said repeatedly, can do that. When the wheels of a weary life are ready to stop, they will. But, sensibly undertaken, it can keep one vigorous, even patients who have suffered heart attacks. Increasingly, physicians are urging heart attack patients to exercise, moderately at first, and later allowing them to follow more strenuous activities such as jogging and even running. Physical conditioning, it has been shown, may help patients adapt better to restrictions forced on them by various diseases. Although, for instance, training does not affect the actual nature of emphysema, there is a suggestion that patients who suffer from the disease — a condition usually affecting the elderly, one in which enlarged air spaces in the lungs make breathing difficult and impair heart action — show improvement in respiratory efficiency and exercise tolerance as the result of conditioning programs. Also, the functional deterioration associated with advancing age may be delayed in some persons who are habitually active.

The cautionary note in all of this, however, is that one who is not accustomed to strenuous exercise could get into serious difficulty by suddenly embarking on a crash program. If conditioning is treated with the sort of respect it deserves — that is, building it gradually and checking with a physician before serious exercise is undertaken — chances are the exerciser won't wind up like the sedentary office worker who enters the Boston Marathon after a bet in a bar, does a mile in the sun, and drops dead of a heart attack.

STRESS

An aged major league pitcher, Satchel Paige, put it best: "Avoid fried meats which angry up the blood. If your stomach disputes you, lie down and pacify it with cool thoughts. Keep the juices flowing by jangling around gently as you move. Go very light on the vices such as carrying on in society; the social ramble ain't restful. Avoid running at all times. Don't look back — something might be gaining on you."

At this writing, Satchel Paige lives in Kansas City, retired, his actual age unknown. Some say that when he began his big league career with the Cleveland Indians in 1948 he was already in his mid-fifties. With his dipsy-doodle curveball, he might well have been one of the best pitchers in black baseball history.

Paige's records may be found in any baseball almanac, but his six rules for long life don't appear in medical textbooks. Nor will the seemingly ageless athlete probably ever do a guest lecture before a medical school's department of preventive medicine. Nonetheless, Paige's six rules make excellent sense today, what with all the emphasis that health professionals place on prevention.

What Paige was talking about, for the most part, was stress, that broad term that refers to physical, mental and emotional strain or tension. He counsels us to lie down and pacify our stomachs with cool thoughts — a call for quiet meditation to break away from ulcer-causing stress. He tells us to avoid running at all times — which has been interpreted by one physician as not succumbing to unnecessary job pressures and hurrying just for the sake of hurrying. His "Don't look back, something might be gaining on you" is seen as recognition that constantly dredging up the past and neglecting the present can bring on unnecessary worry and loss of hope.

There is no guarantee, of course, that easing of psychosocial stress and a loosening of attitudes are going to add a lot of extra years to our life spans. But, if it's true, as so many physicians believe, that two-thirds of all disorders are caused wholly or in part by how the mind reacts to a multitude of things that happen to us as part of the pressure of daily living, then, like mother's chicken soup, learning how to adapt, learning how to change our attitudes, certainly won't hurt and, according to the specialists in this sort of thing, may help a great deal.

There is ample documentation to prove that a positive outlook, meaningful activity, job satisfaction, and an opportunity to fulfill sexual needs improve both the quality and the quantity of one's years. In the Caucasus, for example, the elderly remain active and respected members of the society they live in. They keep up an interest in life; they participate in it. It is not merely a matter of waiting out their days, as is too often the case in the United States. In Abkhasia, journalist Kyucharyants found that work among the elderly was as natural as life itself. People supposedly well over one hundred dig in orchards, thread tobacco leaves, chop firewood, and hunt game. They do not feel themselves a burden either to their family or to society, and on the contrary are respected for their wisdom, knowledge, experience, tradition and customs. "Young people speak last in their presence," observed Kyucharyants, "others turn to them for advice and they decide all moot questions. All the centenarians with whom I talked claimed they had never experienced melancholy or loneliness and had never lost their mental balance. Moreover, most of these people are very well-meaning, friendly, optimistic and of an easygoing cheerful disposition." Leaf made similar observations during his trip through the region, adding that those who did not work on outside jobs had household duties or responsibility for the care of their great-grandchildren.

Along with keeping active, the kind of work one does also influences vitality and longevity, with some jobs carrying more obvious risk than others. A coalminer is in danger of both contracting respiratory disease, from inhaling coaldust, and dying in a sudden cave-in. A baker runs a risk of overeating, with all of the associated dangers. If you're employed on a job that exposes you to asbestos, mercury, lead or radiation — or you're a deep-sea diver, explosives worker, test pilot, policeman, fireman or heavy construction worker — your job safety rating (and your life span) are on the low side. The statistics also place you among the short-timers if you have a job that exposes you not to physical danger but to internal pressures, such as deadlines and weighty responsibility, or carries with it a life-style that promotes neglect of one's health. A lot, of course, depends in such instances on the kind of personality you have. You may, for example, be the sort of person who can adapt well to stress and the demands of leadership, indeed even thrive on it. But it is known that among those with the highest mortality rates are musicians and poets, critics, journalists, authors and editors. There is, unfortunately, little rejoicing when you consider that Keats was twenty-six when he died, Poe forty, Burns thirty-seven, Chatterton seventeen, Schubert thirty-one, Mozart thirty-five, Mendelssohn thirty-eight and Jimi Hendrix twenty-eight — unless, of course, you appreciate that what one produces is more important, in the long run, than how long one produces.

On a less gloomy note, there are occupations which appear to have a favorable effect on longevity. For example, U.S. Supreme Court justices, who commonly live to be eighty or over, seem to be far ahead on the life expectancy charts, enjoying a twelve percent lower mortality rate than men in the general population. Members of Congress, more so senators, fare nearly as well, with death rates eleven percent below the general male average. It has also been shown that the degree of distinction one achieves in his or her professional life affects mortality rates within the group. For instance, if you've attained a degree of prominence as a senator or attorney, you're not only apt to live longer than people in the general population, but longer also than your colleagues who have not been particularly successful. The same reason given earlier may hold true for this group — a more comfortable and rewarding professional and personal life.

Among the longest-living humans — not counting the Caucasians, Hunzakuts and Vilcabambans — are scientists, physicians, educators and clergymen. Again, the more eminent the members of these groups, the longer the life span. Consider, for instance, clergymen. Popes and bishops, who are at the top of the ecclesiastical line, enjoy especially long life. Among the bishops and archbishops who attended the Council at Rome in 1870, there were 150 over age seventy. Of these, 79 were between seventy and seventy-five, 46 were between seventy-five and eighty, 20 were between eighty and eighty-five, and 5 were over ninety. And this at a time when life expectancy was not as favorable as it is today. Suggesting, then quickly dismissing, the idea that Divine Selection and/or celibacy were responsible, a newspaper account of 1912 noted, "The fact that many monks and nuns confined in cloisters and many tradesmen confined in small shops much of their time have lived to extreme old age only proves, if it proves anything, that in all probability they were endowed with extraordinary staying power to begin with and therefore lived long in spite of their unfavorable surroundings." A recent (1971) study by a Johns Hopkins researcher indicates, however, that piety and regular attendance at religious services may, indeed, bestow something more tangible than spiritual uplift on the church-goer — such as a better chance of avoiding fatal heart disease, cancer or some other malady. Dr. George W. Comstock turned up the unexpected but "tantalizing" information about piety's beneficial effects while studying the relationship of drinking water to heart disease, finding that the risk of fatal cardiac disorder for men who went to church infrequently worked out to nearly twice that for men who went weekly or more often. Eighty percent of the subjects and controls in the study were Protestants. "Piety or the frequency of attendance at religious services had a negative correlation with fatal arteriosclerosis and degenerative heart disease," was the way Comstock put it. Such religiosity also appeared to be related statistically to a dozen other diseases including cancer, cirrhosis, tuberculosis, and respiratory problems and, Comstock added, may be as significant as cigarette smoking. But before you dash off to the nearest church in an attempt to countermand an unfavorable prognosis, a word of caution about instant piety's curative nature: It probably won't help much if other habits and those unavoidable genetic traits cancel it out.

"My guess is that the piety-disease relationship is more a matter of life-style," a Boston psychiatrist told me when I asked him for comment on Comstock's work. "A regular church-goer may be regular in other aspects of life. Therefore, the regular church-goer might have less strain and stress on his or her heart, provided it also involves a good diet, plenty of sleep and many other factors. I doubt that just because you go to church every Sunday means you'll be free of heart disease." Comstock himself agrees that there may be a number of explanations, including life-style, for the piety-disease relationship but, he adds, "Whatever it is, going to church is a very favorable input." We can go back to Cohausen, of the maiden's breath, for another version of prayer's worth: "The celebrated de l'Orme, whose exceptional health at a very advanced age was the object of so much comment, preached the beneficent influence which the vital heat of the body exercised on the health of old men. Only instead of having recourse to intimacy with young girls, he contented himself with prayers to Saint Lawrence, who has the rare faculty of increasing the intense heat of the body." (Lawrence, for those unfamiliar with his place in ecclesiastical history, was a deacon of Pope Sixtus II. Ordered by the Prefect of Rome to hand over the treasures of the church, he distributed them instead to the poor, a move which prompted the prefect to have him burned alive.)

There is another possible explanation of prayer's favorable influence on longevity, one that goes beyond spiritual intervention or habits that go naturally with a devout life. This has to do with differences in brain rhythm, especially the alpha and beta waves, that are known to be related to the aging process. Each of the different wavelengths — alpha, beta, theta and delta — is associated with some mental state. It has been known for some time, for instance, that alpha, tied to a state of relaxed awareness, is generated almost exclusively during periods of deep meditation, prayer and relaxation by Zen and yoga devotees, and by contemplative monks. Beta waves appear to be emitted during anxious moments, delta during sleep and theta in periods of creativity. Alpha slowing is probably the most common finding in persons over age sixty-five, and several researchers believe that the degree of slowup is quantitatively related to decreases in intellectual functioning and memory. Related to all of this is what has come to be known as biofeedback training, a technique in which the mind is used to control the involuntary nervous system. Biofeedback harnesses the body's natural rhythms — brain waves and the autonomic functions such as heart and lung action and digestion — to electronic monitors that enable a person to "see" his or her heartbeat inked out on a graph, or "hear" brain waves in the form of a series of high-pitched beeps. By "watching" such usually unconscious occurrences as blood pressure and heart and lung action and "listening" to different kinds of brain waves, a person can influence physical and mental well-being. One might, for instance, lower blood pressure voluntarily, or even ward off a heart attack, by blocking a potentially lethal stress situation simply by learning to control our responses. Hundreds of scientists are now testing biofeedback techniques, and while there is some skepticism, researchers have demonstrated that its medical potential is boundless. One day, perhaps, biofeedback paraphernalia may find its place on the geriatrician's shelf, enabling those who would thwart the aging process to take a cue from Eastern mystics and train their minds to generate the right waves, lower their blood pressure and body temperature, and relieve a host of stress-related disorders. By learning to live in harmony with our internal functions, and without recourse to drugs, we might be troubled by far fewer of the life-shortening ailments that mark our fast-paced lives.

Various social stresses are also important factors in longevity. We rear our families and suddenly the responsibility is gone and our children move away. Our careers peak or remain at ground level or go into abysmal decline. We tire more easily; we ail and bemoan the fact that fewer and fewer people call us by our first names. We grow older, we may lose our homes because of the loss of income of forced retirement, or we lose our spouses through death and divorce. We become grandparents, and the fairy tales we delighted in reading to our children, stories peopled with old witches and hunchback elves with long, white beards, take on a new, distasteful, meaning when we read them again to the offspring of our own. The stresses that come with all of these things not only can shift our body's endocrine balance to make it more susceptible to disease, but they act as depressors that decrease our ability to cope mentally with all of the problems of aging — loss of position, income, friends, health and cognitive powers. "Every stress," says Dr. Hans Selye, a pioneer in the field, "leaves an indelible scar, and the organism pays for its survival after a stressful situation by becoming a little older." Selye has suggested that we are all born with "adaptation energy," which enables us to adjust to metabolic injury caused by stresses in daily living, among them accidents, disease, malnutrition and worry. When the body experiences stress, it draws on its reserves of adaptation energy; when the reserve dwindles, aging results. Selye has filled laboratory rats with enormous quantities of stress hormone and watched them develop a host of diseases and age rapidly due to their inability to replace the lost adaptation energy. In humans, studies have demonstrated time and again that

social disorganization is not only associated with psychiatric disorder but with increased incidence of stroke
mortality, high blood pressure, coronary disease, and
tuberculosis. The individual's physiological ability to respond to stress is impaired, neural and endocrine inte-
grative functioning breaks down, and cells lose their
functional capacity. Stress can also activate viruses that
lie dormant in the bodies of most of us, a mechanism
that may play a part in the aging process. One of the
more fascinating theories about emotional linkup to disease deals with cancer. While the evidence is far from
conclusive, some researchers have suggested that there is
such a phenomenon as the "cancer personality." At an
American Cancer Society seminar several years ago, two
psychologists discussed such a personality, concluding
that it would represent an uptight, defensive, Middle
American member of the Establishment, conformist and
correct in behavior. The same assessment, the researchers said, seems to hold true for the patient who suffers
from rheumatoid arthritis. "Cancer patients are the
Protestant ethic, the nice guys who are committed to
doing what the next guy does, appearing correctly and
being a kind person," said Dr. Claus Bahnson of the
Pennsylvania Department of Mental Health. Cancer patients also, the researchers found, repressed all unpleasant states — anxiety, depression, hostility or guilt — and
described their childhood experiences as bleak and dis-
satisfying. They perceived their mothers as unloving, un-
protecting, and unrewarding and their fathers as unpro-
tective and nondemanding. The basis for the two
behavioral scientists' assumptions was the relationship of

hormones, which, of course, control various bodily functions, to stress, and the relationship between stress states and changes in the body's immune behavior against disease. "Thus, psychological events, mediated by the nervous system, may influence endocrine and immune reactions related to malignancies," Bahnson said.

The inability to cope with stress also brings on a state of social withdrawal that can affect the longevity and health of those forced to live alone, without family or friends, by according them a higher rate of alcoholism, suicide and multiple accidents. Loss of spouse, for instance, can cut longevity. One study in Great Britain found a mortality rate forty percent higher among 4,500 widowers in the year after their bereavement than among married men in the same age category. Nearly half the deaths in the study, which stretched over nine years, were due to heart disease. Behavioral specialists know that emotional stress alone is often enough to cause death since it changes the pulse rate, blood pressure and cardiac output. And should a patient have a preexisting hypertension or heart disease, the danger is heightened. In another study in England, it was discovered that the mortality rate of survivors who participated in the terminal care of family members at home was less than half the rate of survivors who lost a family member in a hospital or other institution. "The resolution of the meaning of death and participation in family structure during the dying process," says Boston oncologist Dr. Melvin J. Krant, "may well be a potent force in determining health patterns of those who continue living." In still another survey, researchers found that a

group of older people who were forced to relocate because of urban renewal, increases in rent or because
their homes were condemned for health reasons, suffered
increased morbidity and mortality. In addition, when the
persons anticipating relocation were examined, they had
elevated blood pressure. Blood tests also indicated either
a reduced food intake to the point of near starvation, or
exhaustion of the adrenal gland, the organ important to
how the body responds to stress. Furthermore, when
compared with old people not facing relocation, the
study group had far more hospitalizations for physical
illness and psychiatric depressions, as well as a higher
mortality rate.

There is a good deal of other evidence that a worth-
while existence has a positive effect on survival. Studies
conducted by Duke University over twenty years indicate that elderly people with stimulating projects are
happiest and actually live longer. In one Duke survey of
270 volunteers between the ages of sixty and ninety-four,
Dr. Erdman Palmore found that those who were satisfied
with their work and were optimistic in their attitudes
lived longer than those who were pessimistic about their
jobs. One eighty-one-year-old man who participated in
the study is a good case in point. His actuarial life expectancy was 5.6 years, and he was in average health.
Because his work satisfaction rating was the highest possible, he was expected to survive 9.5 years. However, he
lived another 11.6 years, more than double the actuarial
prediction. Take life in a nursing home, where being old
all too often means being useless, looked after, just waiting it out. Time and again, it has been shown that when

residents of these places are urged to dress and feed themselves and to engage in activities instead of remaining in bed to be waited on, they live longer. In one Canadian study, sixty-four percent of the active group in a nursing home was still alive after a special program of activities was begun — compared to forty-five percent of the inactive group. Moreover, a good many of the active group had improved so much they were discharged, whereas only five percent of the inactive patients were allowed to leave.

Exactly how many years might be gained by doing away with psychosocial stress, by adopting a positive outlook, by meaningful activity, is difficult to say with certainty. That depends, of course, on many factors, none the least of which is the general state of health. But mind and body, as we have seen, are so intertwined that what affects one often affects the other, whether it be the effect of exercise on mental health, or the effect of a calm mind on a queezy stomach. It is well known that terminal cancer patients — who are usually treated as if they were already dead — can survive for an appreciable length of time if their lust for living is not diminished. "If you don't fight to stay alive, you just aren't going to make it," says one specialist in the psychosocial care of the dying.

The fight, however, requires other participants. Caregivers can help a patient live longer, or at least better, if they care more and show that they do. An employer can pay more attention to some of the warning signals of depression an employee displays — loss of interest, lowered self-esteem, discouragement, heavy drinking.

There are clues that give away a potential suicide — the sudden putting of one's affairs in order, a seemingly casual expression like, "There won't be a next week," or giving away prized possessions. An employee or friend or relative might need close contact, a kindred spirit who can uplift and let him or her know in different ways that life, despite its chameleon course, is worth living, that spring does, indeed, come back, that it is wiser to anticipate and savor moments than to expect and demand sheer bliss every day of our lives.

Insofar as our own lives are concerned, there are warning signals there, too, clues to how long and in what condition we will live. There is, for instance, the category the heart specialists call Type A. That is, uptight, easy to anger at a slow driver who is holding up traffic, overreacting to a child's spilt milk, driven to succeed at the price of family and leisure time. Type A personalities are at risk because their hearts are. There are the chain-smokers, the heavy drinkers, those who wolf down their meals without tasting.

There is no guarantee, as we have said, that altering our life-styles will enable us to live longer. Indeed, there may be individuals who would wither and die sooner if their lives were suddenly tranquil. But we cannot escape the fact that disease and depression, which can shorten our lives, can often be overcome — just as they can be touched off — by our own attitudes and those of the people around us.

Chapter Twelve

I shall be telling this with a sigh
Somewhere ages and ages hence:
Two roads diverged in a wood, and I —
I took the one less traveled by,
And that has made all the difference.
        — "The Road Not Taken," Robert Frost

THUS FAR, WE HAVE concentrated on the ways life may be extended by both biological and evironmental manipulation. But there is a vast difference between living longer and living healthier longer, and one can go back to Greek mythology for an analogy in the tale of Eos and Tithonus. Eos, daughter of the Titans Thea and Hyperion, was the goddess of dawn, the "rosy-fingered Morn" who loved all that was fresh and young. Attracted to the Trojan Tithonus, she carried him off and asked Zeus to give him immortality, neglecting, however, to add to her request, "and eternal youth." Tithonus grew old and helpless, and Eos, to avoid the sight of his infirmity, shut him up in a chamber where, it was said, he turned into a chirping grasshopper.

Eos has her counterpart in American public policy toward the elderly — actually a non-policy that regards old age as a regret, a dubious prize for putting up a game struggle through life. The generally sorry state of the elderly now in our midst — for whom an extension of the mean life span through genetic engineering, enzyme elixirs, or antioxidants will never be possible — the emphasis on all the wrong solutions to their problems (retirement villages and hobbies, to name two of the most fashionable), and their increased vulnerability to everything from crime to suicide cannot be repeated enough. There is always the danger that overemphasis on a laboratory approach to their ills, or attempts to add a few more years to their lives, will see them the losers in a crossfire of competition for dollars between basic researchers who cannot concern themselves with the individual and "service-oriented" agencies that often spend more on public than human relations.

Merely increasing the life expectancy and swelling the population with elderly people without a concomitant solution to the major physical, mental and social ills that beset humankind is, of course, of questionable desirability, and it is doubtful that any of us would opt for a life of senility, or a prolonged terminal stage of disease, over a merciful death. "The way most Americans spend the last years of their lives does not make me enthusiastic about additional years of life until their circumstances are markedly improved," observes one government specialist in aging. "Because life can be extended does not mean it should be extended. It's easy to see how the public and its leaders can slide right by this decision until it is too late to confront the moral issues inherent in it."

There is little doubt that formidable difficulties would be encountered if science succeeds in adding measurably to the life span. Already, the proportion of elderly has better than doubled since 1900. There are, today, some 23 million people over sixty-five in America, and this number is expected to rise to 42 million by the year 2020. In that year, the graying of America will be more pronounced, for one of every five will be over sixty-five. If nothing is done to improve the quality of care for this segment of the population, if no physicians are trained specifically to do geriatric medicine, it will mean more people who have acute medical problems. People blinded, maimed, crippled, or retarded at birth or during their youth would find themselves sentenced to a longer term of pain and discomfort, with all of the drawbacks for work and leisure that such damage would bring. Even now, three out of four of our elderly have at least one chronic disease, one out of four has some degree of hearing loss. And not one single U.S. medical school requires its students to routinely rotate through nursing homes, even though there are now more people in those homes than in hospitals, and more than a fourth of all drugs taken are taken by the aged.

The psychosocial problems of a neglected geriatric society could also be formidable, considering the overloads on food, housing, employment, medical care, pension, and old-age assistance funds that would result. A few years ago, Dr. Alvin I. Goldfarb, a psychiatrist at the Jewish Home and Hospital in New York, painted a rather bleak picture of how a fifteen- to twenty-year increase in life expectancy might be overshadowed by harmful or troublesome psychosocial effects. His gloomy forecast anticipated more physical, geographical, and emotional "distancing" among families, leading to feelings of isolation and self-pity, which in turn heighten depression; he mentioned an increase in mood disorders and problems of middle life with declining virility, changes in appearance, involuntary retirement, fear of loss of masculinity and femininity. Alcohol and drugs, already an increasing problem among the elderly, supply the comfort that society neglects to provide. "There probably will be more depressed, paranoid, socially disturbing and mentally impaired old people in the future," Dr. Goldfarb remarked. "They will be socially unprotected, personally inept and in need of care." It might, therefore, be advisable, he said, to put off extending the human life span for a time. "Until individual reaction and psychosocial response to a changed life span become known, its introduction might tend to increase disastrously the disruptive results on our society of mental disorder and impairment, of asocial or antisocial ways of life, and of poverty. It is even possible that ways of life presently regarded as normal and healthy will, if they become more numerous, be overwhelmingly destructive to our society."

There is also the prospect that as advanced industrialized societies become more and more "aging" societies, they will also become "gerontocratic" societies, with a growing number of power positions held by older people in the judiciary, legislative and economic institutions. Practical knowledge increases with age and experience, and the fruits of this may be resented by the young. Certain new antagonisms may be directed toward the old just as they have been directed in recent years toward youth, who seem to have the world in rein. Covert attitudes toward the aged — such as the reticence to provide them with meaningful roles and raise their status — may become more overt if science is able to extend our healthful and vigorous years so that a person of eighty-five or ninety may be as active and productive as someone of forty.

Dr. B. L. Neugarten of the Committee on Human Development at the University of Chicago has addressed this point, saying that future generations of old people will be different from our present elderly. As we become better educated, healthier, longer-lived, more visible as a leisure class, more accustomed to direct political action and the politics of confrontation, we may also become a more demanding group. Dr. Neugarten has called this phenomenon "ageism." It is not, he explains, apt to take the virulent form of racism because there are biological, psychological and sociological bonds between the generations. Nevertheless, he feels that future forms of ageism toward young and old and the relations between age groups may well be one of the "sleeper" problems of our times, perhaps in the way that race relations was a similar problem a few years back when the urgency of the issues was only dimly recognized by social scientists.

"It may be an exaggeration to compare age-relations,

but at least one observer has suggested that the Western world may now be entering a century of social change," he says. "In this period, as in an earlier century when the major struggle was for political rights and then in a century in which it was the struggle for economic rights, it is now a struggle for age rights. If so, it may become not only a struggle of the young, but also of the old. Attitudes toward age, the effects upon society of changing age distributions, the transmission of values across generations, changing age norms and the relations between age groups should now become a central area of inquiry not only for gerontologists, but for all social scientists."

Failure to do so not only will negate whatever science is able to do to extend our life spans, but it will be proof that we are indifferent to our own inevitable future. For it is us and our children who will either benefit or suffer from the way we approach aging and the aged today. There must be a clear understanding of the distinction between the two issues of how to *extend* life and how to *live* life. The latter, with fulfilled later years as its goal, is a difficult proposition. Certainly there is no lack of discourse on the subject, but what it generally amounts to is a reaffirmation that successful aging is possible rather than any solid advice on how to attain it. Not to worry, we are told, and be your own person, and forget the past it's tomorrow that counts. We take comfort in Confucius saying that it was not till sixty that his ears obeyed him, and Walt Whitman promising Old Age coming with grace, force and fascination, and all the other pat phrases that, in effect, reassure us that you may not be able to teach an old dog new tricks but there are surely a lot of new tricks that only old dogs can teach you.

Implicit in all of this is that fulfillment in old age will simply come in due time, automatically, on schedule, like nighttime and tide. Unfortunately, such is not the case. It is a fact of life that apart from the physical changes that come with age, most of us will be the same persons we were in youth — bright or limited, bitter or cheerful, withdrawn or gregarious — unless we want to alter the format and take steps to do so. And although genetics and circumstances play a major role in whether or not we have aged successfully, there are some other essentials to be considered, suggestive rather than prescriptive though they be. As Goethe said, "No skill or art is needed to grow old. The trick is to endure it." And enduring it is what successful aging is all about — not postponing it, for that we cannot yet do. The answer to how to live life to its fullest is, as we have said, difficult to come by. As elusive as a wreath of smoke, as hard to find as the back of the mind, the answer may well be buried in the spiritual and cultural wisdom of the human race. We are not about to distill it here, but it has much to do with striking the proper balance between two needs — change and continuity with the past — and, above all, learning to forget the clock that ticks away in all of us, and to quit worrying about how long we will live.

But first it is imperative that we examine just how it is we ourselves feel about growing old, though many of us many not be there yet, and how we feel about the aged in our society. Generally speaking, our view of aging is not a positive one, not much different from that expressed in the *Passionate Pilgrim,* in which the writer laments:

> Crabbed age and youth
> Cannot live together.
> Youth is full of pleasance
> Age is full of care;
> Youth like a summer morn
> Age like winter weather
> Youth like summer brave
> Age like winter bare.
> Youth is full of sport
> Age's breath is short
> Youth is nimble, age is lame
> Youth is hot and bold
> Age is weak and cold;
> Youth is wild, and age is tame
> Age, I do abhor thee
> Youth, I do adore thee.

Duke University's Palmore has documented another aspect of negative attitudes toward aging by examining the humor that is aimed at the elderly. Taking a cue from Plato's remark that "humor reflects basic attitudes," and from a statement by the Greek philosopher Jamblichus that "comedy emphasizes the ugly in order to demand a change for something more preferable," Palmore studied hundreds of jokes about old people. In more than half, he found reflected a negative view of aging. Those dealing with physical ability, appearance, age concealment, old maids, mental ability, retirement and death were also mostly negative. The most frequent joke subject was longevity, followed by physical ability, sexual ability and age concealment. Nearly all of the age concealment jokes dealt with women, with the ones about older women more negative than those about older men. For example, the term "old maid" has a harsh connotation, but there is no corresponding negative term for men — "old bachelor" doesn't have the same insulting insinuation.

The one-liner, "My wife hasn't had a birthday in six years," is illustrative of the type of comments about age concealment. In some jokes, an old maid was referred to as an "evaporated peach," or a "lemon that has never been squeezed." Retirement jokes were equally divided between positive and negative attitudes. One with negative implications is about the mother who told the elderly teacher that her son was unhappy because he had to remain in school until he was fifteen. "That's nothing," snapped the teacher, "I have to stay here until I'm sixty-five."

Definitions of age also reflect society's general attitude toward old people. For example, "Age is that period of life in which we compound the vices that we still cherish by reviling those we no longer have the enterprise to commit." There are other examples:

• On longevity: "You are as old as you feel but seldom as important."
• On happiness: A ninety-year-old man was asked

how he felt. "Great," he said, "when you consider the alternative."

• Death: As two old men watched a friend being buried, one observed that they were both ninety. "Hardly worth going home, is it?" the other remarked.

Such attitudes as are reflected in the foregoing obviously do not provide any meaningful role for the elderly. For what they expect most is not an extra thousand years but an opportunity to be useful, to be allowed to continue their personal development. They do not want the pity they get, pity that by its very nature separates us from those at whom we direct it. There is no reason, for instance, why elderly people in good health cannot live alone. There is a resilience that comes with age, a considerable reserve of inner strength that hangs on despite society's neglectful attitude and the pressures of poverty and ill health. In fact, contrary to what most of us believe, ninety-five percent of the geriatric population of the United States is not institutionalized. True, many of the elderly suffer from age-related disorders — but it is also true that they usually see a doctor for the very same problems that afflict younger patients. And while the number and the complexity of those problems do increase with age, the fact is that they can be treated successfully, just as they can be in the young. Open heart surgery, for instance, is not uncommon in the elderly, and neither is the beneficial effect of medication in the treatment of mental decline.

Our attitudes toward retirement are another example

of the ingrained negativism associated with growing old. For many Americans, retirement represents a loss of prestige, social contacts and financial independence. Moreover, we do not enjoy leisure time simply because we are afraid to quit working. "Leisure is a very difficult thing in our society because we don't teach people what it is or how to achieve it," says Dr. Charles White, director of gerontology at the University of Texas. "Instead, we spend 19 years or more preparing them for a job, and when they are not working they just don't know what to do with themselves." Leisure also suffers from erroneous definition — when it is defined at all. It is not watching television or lying on a beach. It may, in fact, involve work. For example, says White, if you are a golfer you may "work" at improving your game — but it is still leisure because you're doing it for your own satisfaction and for the sake of the sport. Your reputation and salary are not in jeopardy, so you can still relax and have a good time. Leisure, then, is a state of being that must be pursued as an end in itself. It is not laziness or idleness.

Among the cultures which have learned to regard retirement as a reward rather than a sentence are the Chinese. Their family structure, religion, economy, attitude toward retirement, even their literature, prepare them for old age and leave them with a role in society. The falling hairs are not a curse. "They are all gone and I do not mind at all," wrote a Chinese poet a thousand years ago. "I have done with that cumbrous washing and getting dry. My tiresome comb forever is laid aside. Now I know why the priest who seeks repose frees his heart by first shaving his head." Said another, "Between 30 and

40, one is distracted by the Five Lusts. I have put behind me love and greed, I have done with profit and fame. Still, my heart has spirit anough to listen to flutes and strings. At leisure I open new wine and taste several cups."

A few years ago, a study in Boston's Chinese community underscored the successful aging achieved by the Chinese, pointing out that the Oriental lives for and in terms of his or her family. By contrast, American families live in different households, with the older generation deprived of the opportunity to share in the problems and joys of the younger. Thus, the American parent, when faced with aging, changes from a needed parent to an outgrown one. Religion, which for the traditional Chinese stresses the importance of family and ancestors, also has much to do with the success of the Chinese aging process. "Confucianism is the worship of one's ancestors by honoring them through improving the condition of the family and maintaining its patterns and its unity," according to the physicians who conducted the Boston study, Drs. S. C. Chen and Joyce Liu Chen. "The aged are a family's closest connection with its ancestors. Thus, the closer one comes to death, the more honored is one's role. For example, presentation of a coffin or burial clothing, called 'longevity robes,' to one's aged parents is considered an act of filial piety." On the other hand, the religions of the Western world, Judaism and Christianity, are monotheistic and religions of the individual, encouraging people to rely on themselves and to be independent of the family and parents. "God helps those who help themselves," is one example of the emphasis on self-reliance. And not so long ago, we sat in a church and heard a priest tell us to give up and pray for our place in heaven, to forget the lust of life and the land of the living and long, instead, for the land of the dead, where it will all be easier, with no one to worry about but ourselves, and that won't be a worry because there isn't any worry there.

What Chinese society is not afflicted with, it is comforting to note, is the prejudice called ageism which pets and patronizes and tolerates the elderly in America, treating them like children who are to be seen but not heard. Many of our so-called care-givers avoid them altogether, as though they had leprosy, or when they are forced to help out of guilt or direct order, become frustrated when their patient does not respond quickly to treatment. Waste, they knew it all the time, what's the use treating a crock? Ultimately, they abandon this person who was once as young as they, dismissing their complaints as inevitable, the natural consequence of the process of aging. Probed and prodded by nurse and intern, the old, frightened and bewildered, most often suffer the added indignity of hearing a mere child in white, made adult by stethoscope dangling, chide with, "Come on now, at your age you can't take this?" And so our aged become hopeless and apathetic, and the quality of the life they are forced to live is low. Not so in the land-based agrarian society of China, where old people have an honored position because their past experience makes them valuable to the younger generations. According to the Chens, industrialized Americans admire progress, progress that is usually associated with ad-

venturous and youthful minds. Most of the Chinese included in the survey were hesitant about being inter-
viewed, while the opposite was true of the elderly whites
in a nearby settlement house. Not only were the whites
more receptive but they tended to be more boastful
about their past, perhaps because they felt their better
days had gone by and they could only look backward to
find pride and satisfaction. The Chinese, on the other
hand, did not conjure up past glories, presumably because they had accepted aging as the time to enjoy the
fruits of a hard earlier life. "Most Americans feel empti-
ness if they lack a hobby started before retirement, because they miss a fast-tempo life in a mechanized age,"
the Chens concluded. "The Chinese does not feel the
necessity of taking up time every minute. If he is a peas-
ant, he welcomes the chance to sit back and relax when
forced to retire because he has worked hard every minute of his life. If he is a member of the gentry, he probably had leisure all his life, so free time is nothing new to
him on retirement."

China's traditional high regard for the elderly is mir-
rored by Japan where, according to Duke's Palmore who
took a sabbatical there, eighty percent of the elderly live
with their children (compared to twenty percent in the
United States). He attributes the considerable respect
for the aged largely to the Buddhist and Confucianist
ways of life, which are daily practiced and not restricted
to one day in the week as church services in the U.S.
generally are. Palmore also found that most Japanese
companies begin retiring workers between the ages of
fifty-five and sixty, which means that the worker gives

up seniority and tenure and often changes to a less demanding temporary job. Fully ninety-eight percent of
Japanese workers continue some type of employment for
another ten years or more, and once finally retired they
become productive in the home, doing housework, raising gardens and tending to grandchildren or great-
grandchildren. "In Japan, respect is demonstrated by the
aged by bowing and by using honorific language," observes Palmore. "Obviously, these are the kinds of practices which would not be adopted in the United States."

We should interject here that the attitudes of U.S. elderly themselves differ enough from those of their Asian
counterparts to make emulating Oriental ways undesirable as well as alien. Take, for example, the matter of
the elderly living by themselves. Many sociologists believe that if young people just out of college and high
school are capable of doing it, then why not a seventy-
five-year-old? Says Ethel Shanas, a sociologist at the
University of Illinois: "All the evidence, both in the U.S.
and in other Western countries, indicates that what
older people want is intimacy at a distance. Old people
want to be near their children, to be able to see them
and their grandchildren, but old people want privacy,
too." There is also no evidence that having older parents
living under the same roof with their adult children
guarantees happiness for either or both parties. "Furthermore, in this age of the automobile and the tele-
phone, it is absurd to assume that physical separation
means abandonment or neglect. I should like to para-
phrase a fellow social scientist and say, 'The number of

hours it takes to go from one place to another is not an index of neglect.' "

While it is relatively easy to accept the idea of the elderly living alone — if only because it shifts responsibility for their well-being from us — it is not as easy to resign ourselves to their sexuality. For though it is well known among gerontologists, and the elderly themselves, that sexual activity and interaction are among the important factors that make the aging process easier to tolerate, the notion is widespread that sex is only for the young, whatever that nebulous collective noun is supposed to mean. Many people, including some of the very old, believe that we lose our desire and capacity for sex as the years go by. Or, if we don't we should. There are the jokes that focus on the lack of opportunity for sexual contact. The eighty-year-old spinster who complained to a neighbor that she couldn't sleep because a man kept banging on her door. "Why not open it?" the neighbor asks. "What, and let him out?" the spinster replies. The ninety-year-old man who died four days after he married a twenty-year-old girl and it took the undertaker four days to wipe the smile off his face. Or the centenarian who says his idea of a happy death is to be electrocuted for rape. Even Napoleon complained, sadly, "At fifty, one can no longer love." Worse is the disapproving attitude of sons and daughters whose aged parents, left without spouses, begin to date again. Too often, an innocent pat on a female child's head, bestowed by an elderly gentleman who needs to touch just as a mother needs to hug a boy, is viewed as the aberration of a dirty, old man.

Whatever the reasons behind such judgmental attitudes — and they probably have as much to do with the way we generally regard our aged as they do with the overly cautious American attitude toward sex — they serve only to reinforce negative feelings about the elderly and impose restraints on them that harm more than help. It is but one more way the road to successful aging is blocked. The Pepsi Generation, standing in the way, expecting the elderly to fall into disuse and disrepair.

The fact is that while the ovaries and sperm-producing cells eventually slow down and quit, and male ejaculatory power lessens, the libido does not. The spirit is, indeed, always willing, though the flesh may be weaker. For the male, impotence does not necessarily mean he must abstain from sex forever because much of it may stem from lack of confidence in his ability to perform, as well as from the sheer boredom of being with an uninterested, unattracting partner. There is also a good deal of consolation in the fact that an older man's erection — when it finally comes up — lasts longer than that of a youth of eighteen. For most women, libido actually increases after menopause when they are free of the fear of pregnancy.

In any event, a sexual relationship doesn't always require coitus to be beneficial for the elderly, although regular intercourse does much to improve morale and physical tone in both sexes, just as driving a car charges the battery and helps the engine run more smoothly. Use it or lose it, is the way psychologists characterize sexual regularity. But consider the case of an elderly couple who had lost the ability to touch one another. The man, age sixty-five, was impotent and fearful of embracing his sixty-year-old wife because it might lead to sex, which he felt he could not handle adequately. His wife was aware of his reticence and his reason for it, and she avoided touching him so as not to embarrass him, though intercourse was not as important to her as a simple caress. After a few therapy sessions they learned how to exchange affection by touching, cuddling and caressing without following through with intercourse — although it turned out that shortly after they began noncoital lovemaking, the husband's capacity for erection returned. Says Dr. Harold Lief, an authority on sex and marriage, "The sense of touching is really underdeveloped in most of us. We have been misled by some Freudian doctrine in regard to this. Freud has given us the notion that the only mature kind of sexuality is coital and that all other aspects of sexuality are, in essence, infantile and immature. I want to emphasize that we really have to turn this about."

In another case, a sixty-four-year-old woman was given permission by her failing seventy-two-year-old husband to seek both sex and companionship outside the marriage. "Their own relationship had been a mutually satisfying one in most respects," said Robert N. Butler, who is now director of the National Institute on Aging. "He was able to make the suggestion, and she was able to accept it without anxiety or guilt. She developed new friends but waited until her husband's death to have an affair. However, the freedom her husband had given her released her from anger and resentment during the long years of caring for him."

Again, while it is difficult to say definitely that a healthy sexual relationship can extend the lives of the elderly and improve the expectancy of younger people, it is certain that it won't shorten our days. There is general agreement that if you're married and living with someone, you can add three or four years to your life expectancy. Married men and women definitely live longer than singles, probably because of greater economic and emotional security. Recent statistics indicate that the death rate for single men in the twenty-five to thirty-five age group is double that of married men of the same age, and twice as high among single women in all age groups. Dr. Leaf has called attention to the finding of a Soviet gerontologist that happy marriage and a prolonged active sex life contribute to unusual longevity. In the Russian's study of 15,000 men and women in the Caucasus over age eighty, there were not many unmarrieds. The Russian also found that women in the region who had many children appear to live longer than those who were childless.

Dr. Butler has summed up nicely the value of sexual interaction among the elderly: "At the very end of life, there is the bittersweet sense that every moment is precious, and sometimes the sense that each encounter may be the last. This is most often poignantly felt by older couples who have met and married very late in life. Those who maintain that the sexual salt loses its savor may be expressing the great difficulty inherent in creating, imaginatively and significantly, the second language of sex. It is difficult to master, but it is a beautiful and satisfying aspect of relating that goes far beyond pure biology."

One man of many years who savored his sexual salt was Thomas Parr, a Shropshire husbandman who reputedly lived through ten sovereigns and died at 152 years in 1635. John Taylor, the eccentric English author known as "The Water Poet" (he worked for a time as a waterman on the Thames), published a pamphlet, *The Olde, Olde, Very Olde Man, Or The Age and Long Life of Thomas Parr, the Sonne of John Parr*, the year Parr died. It does much to destroy the myth of "old" behavior.

A tedious time a bachelor he tarried,
Full 80 years of age before he married:
His continence to question I'll not call,
Man's frailty's weak, and oft to slip and fall.
He did fall, again, a story of an intrigue for which
Old Tom was chastised by the Church:
In first wife's time,
He frailly, foully, fell into a crime,
Which richer, poorer, older men, and younger,
More base, more noble, weaker men and stronger
Have fallen into.
For from the emperor to the russet clown,
All states each sex from cottage to the crown
Have in all ages since the first creation,
Been foiled and overthrown with love's temptation:
So was Old Thomas, for he chanced to spy
A beauty, and love entered at his eye;

Whose powerful notion drew on sweet consent,
Consent drew action, action drew content;
But when the period of those joys were past,
Those sweet delights were sourly sauced at last.
Fair Katharine Milton was this beauty bright,
Fair like an angel, but in weight too light.
Whose fervent feature did inflame so far,
The ardent fervor of old Thomas Parr.
That for the law's satisfaction 't was thought meet
He should be purged by standing in a sheet.
Which aged he, one hundred and five year,
In Alesbury's Parish Church did wear.
Should all that so offend such pennaunce do,
Oh, what a price would linen rise unto!
All would be turned into sheets; our shirts and smocks,
Our table linen, every porter's frock
Would hardly 'scape transforming.

Parr, according to the story, took Katharine Milton as
his second wife at the age of 120, and had a child by her.
The year of his death, he was brought to the court of
Charles I who asked him, "You have lived longer than
any other men. What have you done more than other
men?" To which Parr reportedly replied, "I did penance
when I was 105 years old." After he died, his body was
examined by William Harvey, the celebrated discoverer
of blood circulation. Harvey was unable to find any evidence of organic disease. Even Parr's rib cartilage was
not ossified, but was as elastic as that of a younger man.
Thomas Parr was buried in the south transept of West-
minster Abbey, undoubtedly an "olde, olde, very olde

man," although there is a lack of solid evidence confirming his assumed age.

No one really knows why old Tom Parr lived so long, but I rather suspect that while it was Hayflick's limit that finally spelled his end, he was able to take advantage of every moment in that built-in clock — by an extraordinary resistance to disease, by virtue of being a farmer who did considerable physical labor, and, yes, because "love entered at his eye." It would seem that old Tom had it all going for him — good seed, exercise, and a positive outlook.

The last, positive outlook, is vitally important to a graceful old age. And the warmly personal observations of the elderly themselves attest to this. "Being old can be joyful," writes one resident of a nursing home. "But if you stay in bed a long while you miss out on all the fun others are having. I'm slower moving but I still look after my plants, and I love that. The thing to remember is that if you want to feel proud, do something yourself. Just sitting with nothing to do makes a person glum and he becomes sicker." Talk with the elderly and ask them about growing old, not for their recipes, and many will express similar sentiments, things like, "If you laugh a lot you forget the things that bother you" and "The best is yet to be" and "Being with other elderly folks is better than being by yourself" and "The best way to stay young is not to always think about being old." Or, they tell you that if you want to stay young, have young people around and make new friends, and you'll still feel like you're wanted, and if you have so much to do you won't have time to be old.

Sadly, the public and its legislators do not appear to be aware of such sentiments, and much of the legislation that has emerged for the elderly is directed at those who are chronically ill. There is such a thing as healthy old age, but neither legislators nor medical students are exposed to it in the same way they are exposed to healthy babies in sunny well-baby nurseries and clinics. As Dr. Butler has put it: "One wonders whether medical students would choose to be pediatricians if they only saw babies suffering from irreversible conditions."

Given the fact that healthy old age is a reality and not a myth, it behooves us all to try to develop or enhance certain personality traits that the gerontologists say are necessary for a longer and more comfortable life, idealistic though they may be. Dr. Daniel T. Peak of Duke believes there are five such traits, and they are worth listing here. The first is flexibility and being able to allow changes to occur. This implies the ability to "glide easily" from one activity to another within one's daily life, as well as when preparing and carrying out major transitions in life. Examples of this would be moving from work to retirement, from mother to career woman. Such flexibility within one's self, Peak says, can be cultivated if we realize its importance. The next trait is awareness of one's limitations. This allows a person to utilize his or her capacities in the most efficient way. Self-assessment like this is generally learned by trial and error and though this is inefficient it can be achieved if proper attention is brought to bear. Next is accumulation of knowledge which, according to Peak, should be an ongoing process, involving more than formal information-gathering. It also comprises being worldly-wise by having been exposed to a wide variety of experiences, with life itself as the teacher. Becoming knowledgeable in all areas thus increases the range of one's options, and is a trait that can be developed throughout life, barring accidents or degenerative processes. "We have only recently accepted the fact that 'old dogs can learn new tricks,'" says Peak. "Many older people are returning to formal education in later years and receiving long put-off degrees in late life. The accumulation of knowledge is in a sense like money in the banks of our minds; these are resources which will be drawn on in later years."

The fourth trait is developing resources, or "socking something away for later years." Although fairly well understood when it relates to economic security, the concept of developing mental resources is not. "We have evidence that people who have been involved in intellectual pursuits to a great degree during their lives preserve cognitive functions to a greater degree for a longer period of time. A reserve appears to be built up. This applies not only to formal education but also to experiential learning which allows us to call up certain previous patterns of behavior when they are needed. For example, we observe the ability of older persons to handle a gradual and accumulating series of losses which ultimately includes the greatest loss of all, one's own life. Through a process of having been faced with such minor losses, ways for handling these and greater ones are developed. Some people call these minor grief reactions, or in some cases the development of coping mechanisms. This implies, of course, that one is successful in handling such losses, and if one is not, it may lead to problems such as depression which are so common in the later years."

The last trait is the ability to achieve a sense of well-being. This, Peak believes, should result naturally from the successful development of the other traits, since any well-functioning system leads to feelings of satisfaction, pride, and accomplishment. "However," he says, "I deal every day with people who have never found, or who have lost, the ability to 'feel well.' This feeling of well-being is, of course, intangible. It is not something found in a pill or bottle, as some people believe, but it results from the total interaction of one's personality with his environment."

Does all of the foregoing, all of the emphasis on improving life's quality and altering the mocking stereotypes about aging, mean we ought to totally reorder our priorities? Should the quest for an *elixir vitae* or a cure for the degenerative diseases be put off? Of course not, provided the implications of what we do are fully appreciated, and compensatory steps taken. Observes Leonard Hayflick: "If we have learned anything in the past decades, it has been that we as scientists must be accountable for our activities and specifically responsible for assessing the impact our actions might have on human life if we reached our research objectives. This accountability should go as far as requiring a formal expression of objectives at programmed levels. We now require environmental impact statements prior to letting construction permits. In a similar manner, moral and ethical impact statements should be considered prior to launching research programs that bear directly on the human condition."

Not everyone is convinced, either, that an extension in years will automatically mean calamity, or that there ought to be a moratorium on further research, either out of fear of increased demographic and sociobiological problems, or out of a sincere belief that humans have already reached their ultimate longevity. USC's Bernard Strehler — who believes that the notion that the human life span cannot be increased is "arrant nonsense, an unwholesome adaptation to unpleasant reality" — is one. "If senescence is postponed," he says, "then the attendant decreases in function will also be postponed, as will the social burdens they impose." With senescence delayed, there would be a smaller number of physiologically aged people; men and women in their eighties would look and feel twenty years younger, would stay on the job longer and thus make increased contributions to society.

So, the target at which the gerontologists aim is, in the last analysis, worth the shot, so long as every effort is made to utilize the greater average output that should result from stretching the creative years. It is worth it if probing the biology of senescence spins off even one small positive contribution to cultural attitudes toward aging, if it pays for any extra years that are won with a better world in which to live those years. And lastly, it is worth pursuing because if life were longer as well as healthier, we might enjoy it in a less feverish way, and perhaps a bit more selflessly. Says Alex Comfort: "Partial control of human aging is something that is going to happen. Unless we are slothful or overcome by disaster, it's probably going to happen within our lifetime, and some of us will be beneficiaries. Morally, it should be beneficial. Every gain in our ability to stave off death increases our respect for life — our own and others'."

In the meantime, without an *elixir vitae*, the most sensible way to at least partial fulfillment of what Eos forgot to ask of Zeus is to attend to the controllable factors mentioned herein — without too much thought of any sudden significant expansion of years beyond what the actuarial tables predict. For life is a fatal illness, and humankind does not appear to have the potential for physical immortality. Such an ages-old longing ignores, as we have seen, the evolutionary origin of innate factors that limit the life span of every living thing. Eternal life, which would impose a far heavier burden on us all than a doubling of the life span, is not, of course, what gerontology is all about. Neither is it the stuff of aesthetic surgeons and salons — the face lifts, dermabrasions, chemical cauteries, strawberry-and-cucumber wrinkle creams, deep-pore cleansings and skin steamings. These do not extend the productive years, they only mask our infirmities. Nor is it the equipment of the erector set — the monkey glands, the prosthetic penis, the Spanish fly.

And so we have no choice but to grasp for what we can, and not neglect the springtime, for to sit back, rigid of mind, and suck our gums and fold our hands and wish and wish for a hundred extra years and what might have been instead of discovering and learning and doing new things can bring only boredom, depression, and bitterness. Forget becoming Methuselah dying at 969, and Nestor, King of Pylos, leaving this world at 300 after the siege of Troy. It is not so much time measured by the clock that is important to the aging process, but rather inward time, that aspect of ourselves which differs, as Alexis Carrel has put it, as much from the time of the clock as the solar system does from man. Aging is an individual process, despite the inevitability of the same deficiences that will afflict us all, and there are differences in the problems, attitudes, and abilities of the elderly. The rate of aging varies with the individual, and in different organ systems of the same individual. The years elapsed, therefore, are not as true a measure of life as is the passage of inner time, which if channelled correctly, and its rate of flow carefully regulated, will enrich existence.

I particularly like Pierre Lecomte du Noüy's suggestion that it is the fullness of the day that has worth, that gives one a sense of time as either accelerated or sluggish. "From a psychological point of view," remarks the great biologist-philosopher, "the value of a day is not identical for ephemeral insects and for animals that live to be sixty years old. Even for one individual, this value seems to vary during the course of life. Our duration, therefore, would be, in a certain measure, independent of sidereal time. Each human being constitutes a universe in a state of continuous transformation. It is the rate of this transformation which can be considered as a characteristic of our brief duration, of our physiological time itself, inseparable from our consciousness."

Growing old slowly is what it's all about, I suppose,

and I guess we can by doing the only thing possible under the circumstances — living in the now that is always with us, that will never go away. Every so often, when I'm not complaining that my life is better than half over, I think of time that way, as something that doesn't really ever pass because it is. And it's probably not very scientific, but it's awfully comforting to fantasize that if there's always a now it means I'm part of that and not just drifting away with time, into age, into growing old.

And if I need a creed, I suppose it would be this sketch that some physician drew up of the man least likely to have coronary disease, someone I don't want to be: "An effeminate municipal worker or embalmer completely lacking in physical and mental alertness and without drive, ambition or competitive spirit, who has never attempted to meet a deadline of any kind. A man with poor appetite, subsisting on fruit and vegetables laced with corn and whale oils, detesting tobacco, spurning ownership of radio, TV or car, with full head of hair and scrawny and unathletic in appearance yet constantly straining his puny muscles by exercise, low in income, blood pressure, blood sugar, uric acid and cholesterol, who has been taking nicotonic acid, pyridoxine and long-term anticoagulant therapy ever since his prophylactic castration."

So I will not wait for the gerontologists to find the *elixir vitae*, but rather will listen to Robert Louis Stevenson saying, "Old and young, we are on our last cruise. If there is a fill of tobacco among the crew, for God's sake pass it 'round and let us have a pipe before we go." And I will do all I can to keep soul strong though the body languishes, and I hope I will not be looked upon, ever, as a bundle of dried out, cross-linked rubber bands or some other science writer's analogy. I hope, also, that there will always be someone around to call me John.

Index